Palmistry
EVERY DAY

Photo © Sarah O'Brien

About the Author

Alexandra Chauran (Issaquah, WA) is a second-generation fortune-teller. As a professional psychic intuitive for over a decade, she serves thousands of clients in the Seattle area and globally through her website. She is certified in tarot, contributes to Horoscopes.com, and has been interviewed on National Public Radio and local radio stations. Visit her online at Earthshod.com.

To Write to the Author

If you wish to contact the author or would like more information about this book, please write to the author in care of Llewellyn Worldwide, and we will forward your request. Llewellyn Worldwide cannot guarantee that every letter written to the author can be answered, but all will be forwarded. Please write to:

Alexandra Chauran
⅙ Llewellyn Worldwide
2143 Wooddale Drive
Woodbury, MN 55125-2989

Please enclose a self-addressed stamped envelope for reply, or $1.00 to cover costs. If outside the USA, enclose an international postal reply coupon.

Palmistry
EVERY DAY

Your Life's Path
Revealed in the Palm
of Your Hand

Alexandra Chauran

Llewellyn Publications
Woodbury, Minnesota

FIRST EDITION
First Printing, 2013

Book design by Bob Gaul
Cover art © Lawrence Lawry/Photodisc/PunchStock
Cover design by Adrienne Zimiga
Editing by Laura Graves
Interior Illustrations © Llewellyn art department
Photos © Alexandra Chauran and Llewellyn art department

Llewellyn Publications is a registered trademark of Llewellyn Worldwide Ltd.

Library of Congress Cataloging-in-Publication Data
Chauran, Alexandra, 1981–
    Palmistry every day: your life's path revealed in the palm of your hand/
    Alexandra Chauran.—1st ed. p. cm.
    Includes biblio
    ISBN 978-0-
1. Palmistry. I.
    BF921.C43 2
    133.6—dc23

Llewellyn Publications
A Division of Llewellyn Worldwide Ltd.
2143 Wooddale Drive
Woodbury, MN 55125-2989
www.llewellyn.com

Printed in the United States of America

CONTENTS

INTRODUCTION

Why daily palmistry?

Have you ever been frustrated with the mystery of the future? Wishing, for example, that you could simply know which lover would end up being the one with whom you could settle down and spend the rest of your life? After a particularly hard day that makes you wish you had never gotten out of bed, don't you wish you had seen a sign, before leaving your house, urging you not to proceed? Have you wished for clarity about whether it was the right time to sign on a house, get married, have kids, or make any huge, life-changing decision? Look no further than those wiggly appendages on the ends of your arms.

Palmistry, also called chiromancy, includes the study of not only lines on the palms of your hands, but also fleshy muscles and fat on the palms, bone structure and shape of the hand, flexibility, visible veins, skin, nails, and even hairs on both the fronts and backs of hands and wrists. Anyone can use palmistry, for themselves and others, in order to confirm the owner of the hands' personality characteristics and discover the potential of a person's future. Having a system like palmistry to discover spiritual truths is called divination, although palmistry skirts the definition between being a divination system and a collection of omens. Omens are signs seen in nature that predict events, while divination includes manmade tools for fortune-telling like tarot cards and runes.

Why would you want to know your destiny? Don't worry, you still have a lot of control within the framework of your life's path. Think of it like a road map full of one-way streets. Sure, you have to stay on the roads, so your travel through your fate is somewhat limited, but every intersection allows you a choice that will alter your course, perhaps forever. If you can see the forks in the road ahead of time and where they most likely will lead (depending on other future choices, of course), you can decide whether to turn the other way, hit the brakes, or punch the gas.

As many people know, divination is the practice of fortune-telling using tools or a system, and there are several benefits to palmistry over other methods of divination. For one thing, people have been observing changes in their hands as their destiny changed since humans first noticed they had hands. As a result, there are systems of palmistry in many cultures, including the Western, Chinese, and Indian systems that are popular today. Another benefit of the study of palmistry over the course of human history is that nearly every problem that can befall the human condition has been intricately documented. Whatever need you may have, from love to money to obscure medical conditions, you can bet that somebody else had the same problem in the past and solved it with palmistry's help.

The biggest advantage of palmistry is that it is immediately available to you at any time, since your hands are always right there in front of you. Unlike other forms of divination that may require you to haul around a heavy bag of rocks with runes on them, a deck of tarot cards, or a (somewhat fragile) crystal ball, your hands are washable, wearable, and always available. As a bonus, most other people you meet will have some hands of their own to study.

How palms change

But wait a minute—wouldn't self-palmistry get boring? I mean, after all, you've still got the same hands with which you were born. Not so. In fact, your hands look a lot different from the pudgy baby hands of your past, and those changes have meaning in your life. Many of the changes in your hands happen slowly over time, so you might be the last person to notice if you haven't been looking for them. A professional palm reader can easily pick up differences in the same way that a friend you haven't seen for a while might see right away that your hair has gotten longer or you've lost some weight, even when you haven't noticed it in the mirror. This book aims to train you in the art of detecting the subtle changes that palmistry can reveal, so that you can make changes in your life accordingly.

The important principle of checking your palms on a frequent (even daily) basis

Remember that analogy about the road map of your destiny? A palm reading is like a snapshot of that road map, but the palms of your hands are more like a global positioning system (GPS) that changes depending on each turn in the road. Keeping an eye on where you're going can be easy and fun. Each time you make choices in life, your palmistry readings can anticipate and reflect the changes that will come up as a result. Just as the tiniest portion of a fern leaf is a small, fractal representation of the whole plant, nature and the gods made your hands to tell the story of your existence in the universe.

Myths about palmistry

It is a common notion that one gets a palm reading just for fun, provided by some hokey scam artist at a fair, never to entertain the possibility again. This is a myth. Since your palm readings are like a GPS rather than a map you can frame and hang for reference on a wall, you can and should keep checking in order to make the most of their potential.

Another myth about palmistry I often come across as a professional fortune-teller is the belief that palmistry can tell you exactly when you are going to die. I can't tell you how many times a client has plopped down in the chair and demanded that question of me. Now, it is true that there are ways to determine the likely timing of life events on your palms, just like a handy GPS might be able to guess the time it will take to make your commute to work in the morning. But just as you can take many routes to work and there might be unexpected travel delays en route, *there's no way to tell for certain the exact timing of your death.*

Admittedly, many chiromancers have deeply studied the subject of death in the palm over the course of human history. As a result, there is a collection of warning signs and correlations that tend to occur with the time or circumstances surrounding death or serious illness or injury. Those valuable insights will not be ignored in this book; one of the best things about palmistry is being able to steer yourself in a new life direction if you see warning signs. However, remember that the element of choice in your life, as well as the constantly changing palm readings you'll see, confirm that there is no predictable date of death for each individual.

My own father had a palm reading as a young man that determined that his likely death date at that point in time looked to be aged forty-two. However, my dad ended up dying twenty years after that prediction, at age sixty-two. Why the difference? Maybe the palm reader was incorrect or lying, or perhaps my dad made changes in his lifestyle and outlook that contributed to the added decades of his life. Whatever you see in your palm, good or bad, know that you can make decisions in your life to steer it in a new direction.

Aspects that change over the course of years, months, days, or even hours

Now that you know your palm readings can change, what sorts of things can change? After all, you've probably noticed that your hands retain lines and a similar shape under most circumstances. However, check in with your hands on a yearly basis, and you'll notice big changes in the fleshy parts of your palms as you gain or lose weight or water content in your skin, the lengthening and deepening of the lines, or even lines becoming less noticeable as your hands plump out or your skin becomes more moist.

Over the course of a few months, you may notice changes in skin color or dryness. I know that I tan so much in the summer that it seems like I am an altogether different shade. You may even notice that your hands' flexibility seems to change with the seasons. Freckles may appear and the appearance of your nails can change in a few weeks' time.

In mere hours, the temperature of your hands and moisture of your palms can change. The veins may become more prominent or can recede to near invisibility. Pay close attention to small dots or blotches that seem to appear as a result of blood flow, as they can change on a moment's notice and can have significant meanings. Even rashes, cuts, scrapes, or other injuries can be factored into a reading. I've had clients of mine refuse to present an injured hand to me, not knowing that the marks that the external environment have made on a palm can have just as much meaning as the ones that came with birth or growth.

How to check in with
your palms on a frequent basis

I hope I've convinced you that palm readings are quite useful when done more than once. In fact, a palm reading done only once in a person's life can be pretty nearly useless unless you were to plod through life like a zombie. We see a single reading's ineffectiveness through inaccuracies like the one that gave the wrong death age for my father. The more prudent you are, acting on good advice, the more likely you will enjoy a life that negates that *one* palm reading as you avoid the *one* pitfall it had predicted.

So how often should one perform a palm reading on oneself? At the very least, I recommend twice a year. Make a note on your calendar when you change your clocks for daylight savings time to take a look forward and a look back on your palms as well. Changes will be pretty noticeable on a biannual basis, and I think that any chiromancer or any reader of palmistry books should check a couple of times a year. That being said, this book is going to encourage you to push yourself to look at your palms more often to realize even more benefits from palmistry. The goal will be to check your palms at least each morning and evening, but you might find it so useful that you glance at your hands as often as you check your mobile device. Luckily for you, there are no service fees for this metaphysical GPS, aside from your favorite soap and lotions.

One

HOW TO
GET STARTED

Palmistry basics

Before we dive into the changing topography of your palms, we'll start with the basics and learn the anatomy important to chiromancy. Many beginners believe that lines are the only things read, and yes, they certainly are important. I'd also like to introduce you to the important aspects of your fingers and the fleshy meat of your palms. It is time to learn about those fingers, mounts (the fleshy parts of your hand), and the lines that cross them so you can begin to have points of reference.

*Lines: What they are and what they
mean as paths of travel on life's journey*

If the fleshy mounts and flat plains are the topography
of your hand, the lines are the roads that cross it as you
journey through life. Get familiar with the major freeways
that mark just about everyone's hand, even if you don't see
them change much, because they will help you as reference points for the mounts. Just as you might say, "Hey,
didn't there used to be a fast food joint on this corner?"
on your familiar drive to work, seeing things pop up near
the lines on your palm can be noticeable and more easy
to watch. Lines do change, and for some people they may
deepen, lengthen, or lighten and become less noticeable
more quickly than for others. Keep your eyes on the road
with these major lines on the hand:

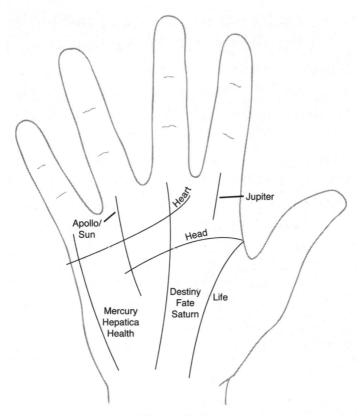

Figure 1: The lines

Heart line: Starting from the top of your hand, the heart line is the highest major line most people have. It starts at the percussive side of the hand, travels through the top middle area of the palm, and terminates under or within one of the mounts. The heart line has to do with your love life, not only the way you seek and find love, but the process of dating and marriage as a journey rather than a destination. Some people have the head and heart line joined as one, which is called a simian crease.

Head line: Under the heart line, most people who don't have lines fused as a simian crease have a head line crossing the middle of the palm, starting near the webbing of the thumb and pointer finger, and traveling to terminate somewhere in the middle of the palm. The head line is your intellectualism, the way you think, and the way you think about thinking. The head line can hold clues about how you interpret the world.

Life line: The life line also starts near the webbing between the thumb and pointer finger and swoops wide around the thumb to terminate somewhere in the middle of the palm or at the bottom near the wrist. Your life line represents your journey through life including health, travel, and living situation.

Destiny line: Many people have a rising line of Saturn that crosses the very middle of the palm vertically, starting somewhere near the bottom of the palm and rising up to terminate somewhere near your middle finger, or at least pointing vaguely in that direction from the middle of the palm. Don't freak out if you don't have a destiny line, as some people do not. This line, if present, has the same associations as the Saturn mount and finger, and often has to do with career and money.

Jupiter line: Some people have a line of Jupiter rising vertically underneath the pointer finger, having to do with
leadership roles and other associations with the Jupiter
mount and finger. This will be explored later, in chapter 4.

Apollo line: Some people have a rising line of Apollo vertically under the ring finger, having to do with the way
they seek recognition and creative influence in the
world, along with other Apollo mount and finger associations that will be mentioned later.

Mercury line: Some people have a rising line of Mercury
vertically under the pinkie finger, having to do with
communications with others, roles in their families, and
helping others in their community, along with other
Mercury mount and finger associations you can read
about later in this book.

Fingers: Put your finger on what they mean

Your fingers are like little peninsulas that jut out from the island
of your palm. They are extensions of yourself, and their length and
shape will be examined later in this book. For now, don't forget to
look for the marks that were described in your morning checks
on your fingers as well as your palm. It is easy to overlook your
fingers, but they have meaning as well, and a mark found on a
finger is just as important as a mark found on a line in the middle
of your palm.

The names of some palmistry aspects may be intriguing to mythology buffs but confusing to new palmistry enthusiasts. Since Greek and Roman philosophers wrote the largest bodies of lore on the Western palmistry system, they got to name everything. As a result, palmistry retains a blend of Greek and Roman names.

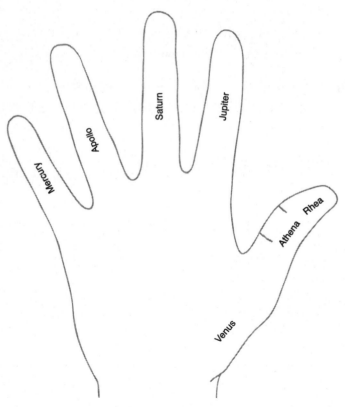

Figure 2: The fingers

Thumb: Your thumb represents your force of will. Ancient palmists thought it visually represented a phallus, yet its three phalanges are associated with the three goddesses, to balance out the gods of the other fingers. They are Rhea, Athena, and Venus respectively, from tip to base. If your willpower is being affected by something today, you may find a dot appearing on it. Other marks can be warnings representing a test to your strength of will coming up, or they can be blessings lending force to your inner strength. I like to remember it this way: when hitchhiking, you want to go somewhere; think of your thumb as a representation of your desire to go and do things, or to be yourself.

Pointer finger: Your pointer finger is called your Jupiter finger. As Jupiter was the ruling Roman deity, equivalent to the Greek Zeus, think of this finger as relating to your own leadership skills and your relationship with authority figures. Your Jupiter finger has some information about your drive for success, often in business, so think of your pointer finger as your assertiveness when pointing the way you want yourself or others to go in life.

Middle finger: Your middle finger is your Saturn finger, also called the "fool's finger" in some older texts. Saturn is the Roman god of justice and the harvest, equivalent to Cronos (sometimes thought of as Father Time). Two rules come to mind: 1. You can't fight time; 2. In time, you reap what you sow. Accordingly, the middle finger has to do with duties, obligations, and rules, often having to do with career and finances. It is easy to remember the middle finger as being associated with a rude gesture, so I like to remind students that no matter how childishly you might want to give the middle finger to your financial needs, you cannot.

Ring finger: Your ring finger is your Apollo finger, having to do with the realm of creativity and the arts. Not only was the sun god Apollo a musician, he also brought light to the world. Since the Apollo finger is thought of as the wedding-ring finger, try to remember that art, music, dance, and creativity are ways you express your heart's deepest desire. Since Apollo was thought of as the god of medicine, ancient physicians would stir potions with their ring finger, thinking that if it were being mixed wrong, the heart would let them know.

Pinkie finger: Your pinkie finger is the Mercury finger, also known as the "ear finger" in some older texts. The Roman god Mercury is considered equivalent to the Greek god Hermes, who wore winged sandals and was the gods' messenger. Likewise, your Mercury finger has to do with forms of communication like the Internet, telephones, signing contracts, making business deals, and even teaching (or manipulating) other people face to face.

Other characteristics: The meanings
of mounts, stars, and more

The mountains and plains
on the landscape of your hand

If you look at your palm from the side, you'll notice that it is lumpy due to the bones, muscles, and skin of which your hand is comprised. The lumps are called "mounts," so think of them as the mountains that make up the map on your palm. The flat or depressed areas are called "plains." Each little hill or valley has its own domain. For example, each mount under a finger joint is connected to the finger above it. So the mount of Jupiter has the same meanings associated with the Jupiter finger. The same goes for the mounts of Saturn, Apollo, and Mercury. What happens if you see a marking that falls in between mounts or on the edge of a mount? Make sure you take into account the meanings of both mounts when interpreting such marks, as their effects may encompass both domains of your life. Here are some other mounts besides your finger mounts, along with the plains.

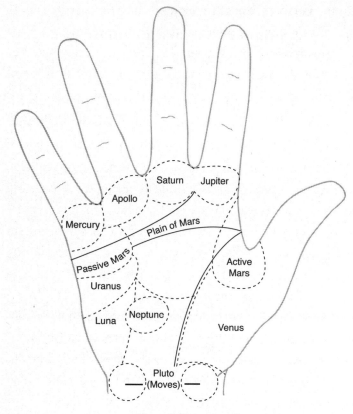

Figure 3: The mounts

Mount of Venus: This is the mount of your thumb and it has to do with love relationships of a romantic nature as well as sexual passion. The mount of Venus is also where your sensual sensitivities lie, even if you aren't currently with a lover. Perhaps redecorating your house is as good as sex for you, in which case positive marks might appear on your mount of Venus.

Lunar mount: Opposite your mount of Venus, on the percussive edge of your hand, is your lunar mount. This area has to do with your very deepest psyche, whether it be filled with spiritual thoughts, dreams both literal and figurative, or even insanity. If you're looking for your subconscious, you'll find it here on the mount of the moon.

Mars: Below, I'll detail the different parts of Mars's domain. You can remember that the whole middle of the hand is the realm of Mars, god of war, because that is where you would grip a weapon. Also, his initial, the letter "M," seems to be written on the palm of the hand with those three major horizontal lines.

Mount of active Mars: The mound on your palm where the web of skin is between your palm and pointer finger has to do with your assertiveness, aggression, temperament, and temper. This is how you present yourself to the world when you have a problem or a goal.

Mount of passive Mars: Just above your lunar mount on the percussive side of your hand, opposite your active Mars is the mount that has to do with how you react to what others and the universe throws at you. This is how you process slights and insults.

Plain of Mars: In the valley between your head line and heart line, in the middle of the mounts of active and passive Mars, is the plain of Mars. If the active Mars is your offense and the passive Mars is your defense, the plain of Mars is the battlefield on which all of those energies and influences play themselves out. You'll see a lot of turmoil and conflict between yourself and the people in your life play out on your plain of Mars.

Mount of Uranus: Sandwiched between your passive Mars and lunar mount on the percussive edge of your hand is the mount of Uranus, having to do with your inventiveness and idealism.

Mount of Neptune: At the inner edge of your lunar mount is the mount of Neptune, involving travel and a bit of your creativity in the sense of building your dreams into reality.

Mount of Pluto: This movable mount is right at the inner base of your palm where it meets your wrist, hugging either your mount of Venus or your lunar mount. It shows big transformations on the way, and can also have to do with sibling relationships.

Smaller, more subtle markings

Now that you've learned the basics about your fingers and mounts, let's get into the rudimentary details without getting overwhelmed. A comprehensive palm reading takes time seated under a bright light, perhaps even using measuring or recording tools, studying each hand carefully front to back, wrist to fingertips. So the first key to using palmistry every day as an effective guide is to learn to check your palm quickly, like you might check a website for traffic delays or outside temperature before getting dressed and heading out the door to work.

To get you started with learning the minor markings on your palm, I'll include some simple checks I think are important to do on a frequent basis. Daily palmistry may be challenging for you at first, but as you become familiar with the palms of your hands, you may find yourself easily adding more aspects to your inspection from other chapters of this book. In the same way that you know your own face in the mirror and can quickly spot signs of fatigue or oncoming illness by observing your eyes, hair, or skin, your palms will become old friends with new information.

Five palmistry checks to make
before you leave the house in the morning

For a quick spot check in the morning, only view your dominant or "active" hand. Your active hand will demonstrate the quickest changes, and is an easier way to attune to the day ahead, challenges at the forefront of your mind, or dangers that might have you cancelling a trip or calling in sick for the day.

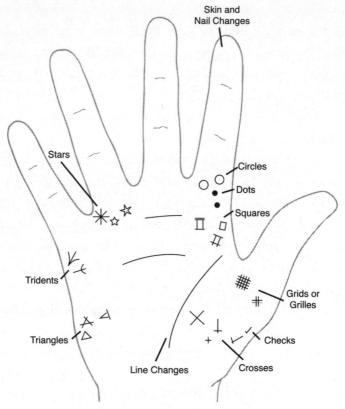

Figure 4: Five palmistry checks to make
before you leave the house in the morning

Colored dots on lines or mounts of the palm

Take note of any subtle or obvious colored regions of your palm, as these are often the most frequent to change. Most often appearing as dots or blotches, these spots may lie over or touching a line in your palm or they may ride high on a fleshy lumpy part of the hand (these are called mounts) or on a finger. More information on interpreting those dots and the significance of their location will be included later in this book, but basically the color of the dot indicates the nature of the sign while the location indicates the domain of life that gives it context.

During your quick morning checks, know that white, yellow, black, or blue dots encourage you to make the day low-key to preserve your energy and health. Mottled, green, or red dots suggest that the day ahead may be intense and exciting, so you'll have to exercise great awareness and self-control. Pink dots are a good sign that you're healthy and ready to take on whatever the day throws at you with relative ease.

Stars, tridents, grids, or grilles

These are all warning wrinkles that may show up frequently on the fleshy mounts or palms, linger for a time and then fade to nothing notable when trials have been overcome. Again, the location of these marks holds context, and will be explored in depth later in this book. Generally, tridents are the most minor, even if they are large or deep, which means that the challenge will be pervasive or long-lasting. A trident is, in a way, a good sign, as it indicates that you have the protection, strength, and resources to solve a problem relatively unscathed. Likewise, grids and grilles are minor signs of an obstacle or unstable foundation.

Stars are the most serious bad omen. It has led some unscrupulous palm readers (gasping, of course, in horror) to reveal a curse that can, of course, be "cured" with a generous pile of money. But in reality I would bet that nobody has made it through life without a few stars making an appearance. If you have a new little asterisk on a mount, don't freak out, but it wouldn't hurt to take a snapshot or make a quick photocopy of your palm. Date it, then go about your day. That way, you can be on your guard and study the implications later. If the star is a huge or deep pentagram or Star of David, and if it has appeared suddenly coupled with known life upheaval, consider retreating to meditation, therapy, or a vacation to strategize and rethink your life. It's okay; you can blame me when you call in sick to work. You can tell your boss that your psychic told you to stay home today.

Squares, ovals, circles, triangles, and crosses

These wrinkles appearing on the fleshy mounts are good signs, which should cheer you up about the day's potential. Triangles are an even more positive version of the trident and show a bit of good fortune that will get you out of a pickle. Similarly, circles show you overcoming a problem by transcending it or solving it at its core by adapting. Squares show your resources of strength and energy that have been made available to you for great things to come. Some people think that squares are bad things because they are limiting, but they often denote positive or necessary limits such as a period of confinement or solitary reflection. A square over a break in a line, especially the life line, is called a "protective square" that helps you through a period of hardship. Ovals show a gift or an ally, and are often associated with women around you or with characteristics commonly attributed to the feminine. A cross, especially a new or obvious one, can be the best sign for someone hoping that an area of life will speed up or become more focused, although it often implies that a compromise is coming with the good fortune.

Deepening, lengthening, shortening, or splitting of lines
Wait a minute; didn't this crease reach to my wrist at one point? What's with this new fork in a line? Was this line always doubled? How come all the lines in my hand today look more noticeable or even deeper? These sorts of changes will take time and experience to notice, and they too may require a quick snapshot or photocopy for later study.

In general, a change in the head line may be asking you to sit up and take notice. Your plans or your way of thinking and communicating have to change. A difference in the heart line means a real relationship change is in store. A change in the life line may be a big tip-off that your health, environment, or occupation could be affected. All of these changes are to be expected if you're going through a divorce, having a child, changing jobs, or even traveling, so don't fret. Just make sure you examine the line changes later for clues and guidance about upcoming life changes.

Changes in the pressure, texture,
or overall color of hands and nails

Are your hands puffy, sweaty, cold, gray, suddenly prone to bruising, or otherwise discolored? You may be coming down with something. Yellowing of the nails or edema (fluid-filled areas) can indicate the development of serious health problems that might require a doctor's attention, while sweaty palms or blotchiness might indicate stress or a cold that just needs a little rest.

Some people's hands get very hot or very cold when in the presence of energy, the life force that flows through all things. Sensing this energy can key you in to others in your household or community that are experiencing high emotion. Follow the clues to decide whether to lie low for the day or explore what is going on with yourself and those around you.

X marks the spot

Thus concludes the quick spot check I would advise you to make every morning. Knowing the regions of your hands is useful when observing minor details because the location of the marks of warning or blessing on your hands can give you more details about what may be in store. For example, a dark grid on your lunar mount may mean that you are becoming emotionally or mentally unwell, while if the same grid appeared on your life line, it would be more likely that you're headed for a more physical sickness or injury. In order to scan your palm for these minor details with points of reference, here is another practical exercise that can be performed daily.

Five palmistry reflections
you should make every night

When winding down at the end of the day, it can be more valuable to reflect on your past and make sure you're staying the course for your long-term goals, rather than fretting about the immediate worries of the coming day. For these nighttime checks before bed, look just at your passive or nondominant hand. This hand shows some of your enduring traits, your past and childhood, as well as your ultimate destiny as it is being formed. Unless you're going through a crossroads in your life that is characterized by major upheaval, most people notice that changes seem to happen more slowly and subtly on the passive hand. However, it is still a good idea to look over your passive hand daily to remind yourself to stay on track with your values and goals, and to see right away if you're getting off course or have initiated a huge change in your life.

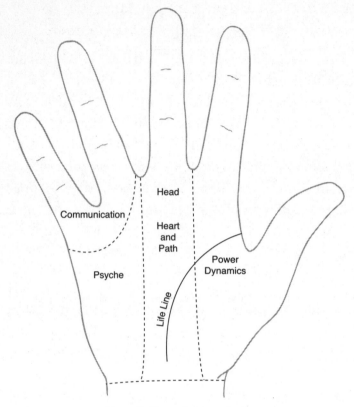

*Figure 5: Five palmistry reflections
you should make every night*

For each area of the hand I want you to check, you can look for the marks you saw in the morning to see if they're still there, affecting that area of your life for longer than just the day. You should also look for changes over time. These changes may be deepening or lengthening of the main lines on your palm or a shallower and less pronounced look to the lines. Deeper lines mean more energy given to an area of your life; significant change and effort are underway. Think of the lines in your hand as little rivers. If the rivers are deep, they are flowing swiftly, possibly with frightening rapids. If they are shallow and look like little chains, the river of energy may be drying up or diverting the flow elsewhere. Is that what you want? It depends on your goals in life. Take a look at the following areas and see if you're on track.

Check in with your power dynamics. Give yourself the "OK" sign with your passive hand. Now look at everything on your hand that is on the thumb-side of your middle finger. This area of your hand includes your Jupiter finger, your thumb, and your mounts of Venus, Mars, and Pluto. Think of this area of your hand as where most of your give-and-take energies with significant people make their marks. Your finger is an overview of your leadership and relationships; the web between it and your thumb is the active mount holding signs of your assertiveness and temper; the fleshy part of the base of your thumb is a place of love and giving in your life; and the bottom of the fleshy mount where your hand meets your wrist is your Pluto mount, which represents transformation as well as family relationships, especially with siblings.

Are your head, heart, and path in harmony? Look at your middle finger as well as the middle of your palm. In fact, if you were to make an obscene gesture with your middle finger, the areas left uncovered in the middle are what I'd like you to check next. That Saturn finger and any line you may have coming down from it have to do with your job, your duties, and your dealings with authority figures. Below that are your heart line for love; your head line for intellect; the plain of Mars in between them, showing your actions in those two areas; and your Neptune mount, indicating travel or your desires to build something big in your life.

Commune with your communication. Your ring and pinkie fingers, and the mounts just below them, are big communication zones with everyone in your life, including internal communication with yourself. This area differs from those power dynamics areas we talked about earlier such as your Jupiter finger, also known as the pointer finger, and your mounts of Mars and Venus, because they have to do with communicating actual messages rather than the more subtle push and pull feelings in relationships. The Saturn finger, your ring finger, has to do with your self-talk and artistic abilities. Your pinkie finger is your Mercury finger, and it encompasses all your communications, especially those in business as well as through technology like telephones and the Internet. Just below the Apollo finger is an area to look at for success with your creative endeavors, while just below your pinkie finger is a good spot to check in with communications with your closest family, like spouse and kids.

Attune with your deepest psyche, your spirituality, and the world of magic. The percussive edge of your hand is the part that you would use to karate chop a block of wood. This area is made up primarily of the lunar mount, bordered at the top by the mount of Uranus and at the inside edge by the mount of Neptune. The lunar mount contains your deepest dreams and imagination, while the mount of Uranus includes your inventiveness and the mount of Neptune, as you already checked earlier, includes some creativity. Noticing changes in this area can mean that your spiritual values are in flux, or even that you may be suffering from a serious mental problem or intellectual quandary during a period of personal growth.

Study your life line. The life line is so important to any period of reflection on your path through life that I'd like to include it separately so that it doesn't get overlooked as you check your palm before bed. Your life line is more than just a health indicator. It also holds clues to big shifts in your journey as well as a change in focus or in the way that you do things. Pay special attention to new small branches of the life line and follow where they lead. Any other mounts or lines they touch or to which they point will emphasize the significance of these areas of life or personality traits.

Two

WATCHING
FOR CHANGE

How hands change and
how to note changes in your hands

You will experience subtle changes in your hands' color, skin texture, fat and musculature, puffiness, moisture, and even your lines and skin patterns, from natural markings to scars. It is not enough for me to tell you that your palm readings will change over time; you have to experience the shifting nature of palmistry for yourself. In order to do that, you'll have to be disciplined and make careful observations. Just like any other serious spiritual study like dream interpretation, meditation, or magic, it takes time and consistent devotion to practice to see real results. However, if you give the art of palmistry the respect it deserves, with time, effort, and attention, you will be well rewarded.

Keeping a palmistry journal

The most important way to learn palmistry and to benefit from watching changes over time is to keep a palmistry journal. Not only will you record images of your palmistry readings, but your immediate and later impressions will be preserved as well. As your comprehension of palmistry evolves, and as new revelations come about in your life, only by keeping a journal will you be able to look back and modify your comprehension so that you can better predict the future. Images are important, yes, but the prose writing of your thoughts about what you see is vital to go along with each picture. There are many ways to record imagery of your palmistry readings over time, so I will go over some of them to let you know their strengths and weaknesses.

Even though it seems archaic in this modern digital age, drawing palmistry diagrams is, in my opinion, still the very best way to keep a palmistry journal. If you use no other method to record changes in your palm readings, draw diagrams by hand. What seem to be the biggest weaknesses—a lack of detail and missed observations—are actually the greatest strengths of hand drawing. The limitation of your time and attention allows your intuition to capture the most important aspects of your palmistry reading. Your immediate, first impressions are those from your subconscious, psychic self—those are the observations you should record. Who cares if you can't draw every tiny speck on your palm? If the background noise of your palmistry reading doesn't jump out at you, it is okay to leave it out of your recording or make a drawing and record your palm in another way as well. You don't have to be a great artist in order to make palmistry diagrams. Just as you might sketch out a quick map for a friend to find a destination, being able to see the waypoints on your palm and know what you meant later on is all you need. Again, it is vital to include written words describing your drawing and its interpretation at the time that you made the record.

The second best method for recording your palmistry readings is with a high-resolution digital camera. I suggest you take a digital photograph of the fronts and backs of both of your hands, from the same angle and distance from the lens and under the same lighting conditions, once a month. Since a high-resolution digital camera allows you to see details, you will be able to notice nearly every change over time.

A digital scanner or photocopy machine is a great way to take a quick record without having to worry about lighting conditions (like whether it is the same time of day as the last time you took a digital photograph if natural light from a window affected the picture). Remember to clean the glass on the machine before and after you use it to remove fingerprint smudges. However, a weakness of scanners and photocopiers is that the surface of the machine smashes your palms flat so that you can't see mount changes or depth of lines and, of course, if your photocopier is black and white, you lose all color interpretation opportunities.

In practical everyday life, I use a combination of methods to record my palmistry readings, and so should you. I suggest keeping a palmistry journal and sketching a very rough diagram quickly when you notice changes in your morning and evening readings. Once a month, take a digital photograph of the fronts and backs of both of your hands and make a journal entry comparing the photographs to those of the previous month or year. If you notice a big change in your hands during a morning or evening check, or just during the day at work or wherever you have a scanner or photocopier available, dash off a quick copy or scan of the hand in question so that you can sit down and have a look when you have time to write about it in your journal. If the change you notice is the length of a line, it doesn't matter if you make a black and white photocopy, because it still records what you want to document. Changes in your palmistry readings can happen very quickly, so don't miss a chance to record something that startles you. You might question later whether what you saw was just your imagination.

Noticing differences

Though frequent checks are the key to noticing differences, your observational skill is a learned ability, and not being able to see changes right away can feel very frustrating.

Don't get discouraged! Use recorded images to compare and find the differences. Try looking for changes once a month by comparing your records from the previous month. Place pictures side by side to make a comparison and look back and forth to find the differences, just like in the "spot the difference" games published in newspaper comic sections. You can even circle every difference you see before attempting to interpret the changes. If you don't see any differences, consider using high-resolution digital photographs, if you aren't using them already.

Read through your journal entries for changes in interpretation. Letting your intuition shine through is an important part of noticing changes in your palm readings. Even if the actual features of your palm haven't changed this month, look back at last month's interpretations and see if you feel differently. Perhaps last month a star on your rising line of Saturn made you think you were going to win a dance audition, but instead you didn't do so well and your fame came in the form of getting drunk in front of friends and strangers at a bar. Changing your feeling about the way signs show on your palm is okay, because that helps you learn how your hands are showing your future. Some people have certain signs pop up more often than others, which gain more precise contexts with your experience. For example, if you notice a red dot low on your thumb every time you slip and fall, even if no palmistry book tells you that's the "mystic mark of the clumsy," you will be able to avoid future accidents by being more careful whenever the mark appears.

Overlays

Overlays are a basic palmistry concept vital to using palmistry every day. Overlays refer to a wide array of palmistry features, usually transient or quickly changing, that are different from your normal palm patterns. It is easiest to observe overlays on yourself, because things may look different than usual. For example, the life line on your active hand may suddenly break out in tiny offshoots if you're planning a lot of travel, accompanied by positive marks like crosses on your pinkie finger or the mount of Mercury below it.

Overlays can be noticed on the palm of another by a skilled reader during one session by comparing the passive hand to the active hand, which is more likely to have overlays, or simply by noticing palm features that don't seem to fit the hand type. For example, if a person has a rough, beefy palm with tiny, spidery fingers, the fingers may seem out of place, and an experienced palmist may ask if the person has noticed that he or she has dropped a couple ring sizes lately.

The most common overlay is the "psychic overlay," since many features can point to intuition and since one's psychic ability can ebb and flow according to life circumstances and even the phases of the moon. A psychic overlay often includes, but is not limited to, conic fingers that are long and slender like antennae, many branches from the head line, and perhaps the presence of a mystic cross. If this constellation of features marks an active hand differently from a passive, or appears on a hand that is otherwise quite average, it is considered a psychic overlay.

When you notice overlays on your own hands, make a drawing showing just the features that are new, different, or out of place. Go ahead and leave out the features that you normally see on your hand so that you can just focus on interpreting the overlay. Write down your thoughts and interpretations about what you see, and don't forget to look back in a month's time to see if the overlay has shifted, disappeared, or become more prominent.

Three

TAKING ACTION TO CHANGE YOUR DESTINY

If palmistry could simply tell the future, it would be a neat party trick, but it wouldn't be very useful. It would even be quite scary to see bad things that will happen in the future no matter what you do. Happily, palmistry is much more useful. If you see something bad appearing in the palm of your hand, you can work to change it. Will your hands actually change when you change your destiny? Yes, it is possible! Many people are surprised when I say that you can actually change the way your hands look just by making significant decisions in your life. That's why I encourage you to keep a palmistry journal so that you can see this incredible phenomenon for yourself, and to watch for quick changes—like a red dot on your Jupiter mount below your pointer finger appearing each time you have a headache—so that you can see that palmistry changes really are possible. It is also possible, however, that you will avert a danger in your path and still bear the mark on your palm for the remainder of your life. Just like a healing scar from an accidental close call, you can think of those marks as badges of courage and reminders to be careful to avoid such a fate in the future.

What do significant changes mean?

I'm going to divide the omens you might see in the palms of your hands into positive "go" signs that give you the green light to go about your day or pursue your highest goals, and negative "warning" signs that give you a red light to think about before proceeding. As you read through the examples of significant changes you might see, avoid feeling invincible or doomed; remember that these signs can change under your own power. Following this list of significant changes, along with suggestions as to how to react to them, I'll give you some ways to create change in your life—and in your hands.

Significant changes
on your palm that say "Go for it!"

Palmistry is an amazing tool for confirmation of immediate action to be taken. For example, a cross appearing below the Apollo, or ring finger, is an excellent sign for marriage. Imagine a woman spotting that cross on her hand the morning that her boyfriend proposes. Such a cross can help her erase all doubts from her mind and make the leap of faith that marriage is indicated as auspicious. As a professional fortune-teller, I actually see this sign on hands often, since I am hired for many bachelorette parties as entertainment. Sometimes it is more than just the bride-to-be who has this sign of impending marriage on her palm, so I can guess who is going to catch the bouquet! If you're planning for marriage in your future but haven't yet met the right person or deepened your existing relationship to that point, don't be surprised if the cross on the mount of Apollo shows up on your passive hand. That just means that you're on the right track. For the "go for it" signal, keep your eyes on your active hand.

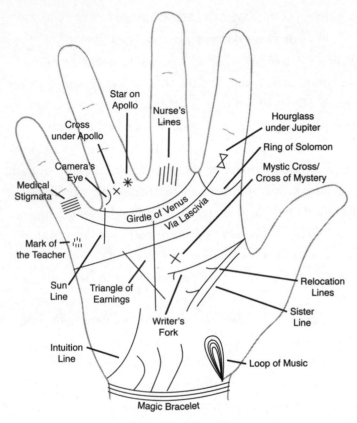

*Figure 6: Significant changes
on your palm that say "Go for it!"*

In general, as mentioned in your morning palm checks, squares, ovals, triangles, and crosses are all good things that give you the go-ahead to proceed with your decisions in life. Pay close attention to the areas on your palm in which they appear, to receive more detailed wisdom about what focus in your life has the most clear path for you right now. Here are some more examples of "go" signs.

Camera's eye: A rising line to Apollo, meaning one that swoops through your mount of Apollo to meet your ring finger. This sign encourages pursuit of the visual arts.

Girdle of Venus: A horizontal line scooping below the Apollo and Saturn fingers tells you to trust your aesthetic assessment of people, places, and things.

Hourglass on your mount of Jupiter: A mutually beneficial relationship is about to begin if this sign appears, so get ready to be fair with your giving and taking.

Intuition line: Starting at the base of the palm on the percussive edge of the hand, the intuition line is a curved line that swoops upward through the lunar mount and may be quite long. A long intuition line that points toward the head line is a good sign for a healing vocation, while a swoop toward the destiny line indicates a good potential career as a psychic or clairvoyant.

Loop of music: If you're going to have a career as a musician, you'd do best to have a loop of music showing your talent. This whorl, like those found on your fingerprints, is found starting at your wrist on the thumb edge of your hand and swirls upward onto your mount of Venus. More about these fingerprint-type markings, called dermatoglyphs, will come in the section on personality characteristics that are unchanging. You can't force yourself to develop a loop of music, so if you don't have one, don't fret over it. Creativity and good business sense are just as important to making musical art a career.

Magic bracelet: Planning a lot of travel? Three deep lines in a row, all crossing the wrist completely are called rascettes or a magic bracelet. A magic bracelet helps with safety and wellness during travel. If a line points from the rascettes to the pointer finger or ring finger, travel will bring fame and fortune. If lines from the rascettes go to the lunar mount, travel will lead to love.

Mark of the teacher: Lines jutting up on the Mercury mount, just below the pinkie finger, promise that you will keep coming back to teaching in one way or another, so go ahead and embrace that role. The teacher's square, which is a square found on or just beneath the mount of Jupiter, is also a positive indication that teaching is the right career for you.

Medical stigmata: Five parallel lines on the mount of Mercury, under the pinkie finger, indicate that you will have luck in the healing arts of any type.

Mystic cross or cross of mystery: A cross found under the mount of Saturn or almost under the mount of Apollo, but sandwiched between the heart and head lines is a sign to trust your intuition and a blessing to dabble in the occult.

Nurse's lines: Above the heart line there may be clusters of vertical lines on the finger mounts indicating a person has healing hands. Nurse's lines are a good sign to see if you are going into a career in massage therapy or other healing work involving your hands.

Relocation lines: Planning a move? Check your life line for small branches appearing. If the branches have a big angle to them, a move far away will be most auspicious, while a tiny angle means you should look for a better home closer to your current neighborhood.

Ring of Solomon: A positive sign for somebody considering a job or volunteer vocation of service or a psychic calling, this is a curved line that cups the mount of Jupiter.

Sister line: If you have another line on the thumb side of your life line, this can be a mark of spiritual protection during this point in your life. If the lines are very close, it can also indicate that you are living two different lives, which can be positive if it represents good roles like wife and mother, but it might get a bit on the warning side if you're spreading yourself too thin.

Star on Apollo: This sign appearing declares a potential for fame. Be careful, as this can be a bit of a warning as well, to make sure that you are famous, not infamous, for your creativity. It is all in the context. If you're working on becoming an actor or a singer, this is a wonderful sign, but if you are not at all working toward fame, this should be a huge red flag for you to make sure you don't appear on the news for doing something appalling.

Sun line: Also known as a rising line to Apollo, and considered to be a sister line to the destiny line, this line's appearance is always a positive sign. It indicates that success can be brought about through your own self-confidence.

Triangle of earnings: The three lines of this triangle are formed by your head line, your rising line to Saturn if you have one, and a special line that can appear to connect those two to form the third side of the triangle. When it is complete, it shows a good potential to hold onto money, while if it is open between any of the lines, it can warn that your money might slip through your fingers. The size of the triangle can represent the size of the sum of wealth.

Via lascivia: This line from the Jupiter finger to the Mercury finger indicates the potential for physical passion and chemistry. It is a wonderful sign to see if you're looking for a new lover or wanting to add spice to your current relationship.

Writer's fork: If you're hoping to get a book published, the existence of a fork at the end of your head line is a great sign to go ahead and take the chance to complete that manuscript and send it in.

Warnings that appear
in the palm of your hand

As mentioned in your morning palm checks, stars, tridents grids, and grilles are all warnings. Spots, especially those markings colored yellow, white, or definitely dark like purple or blue, emphasize the warning. The location of these marks on your palms can show you in what area of life you may need to exercise the most caution. You don't need to be constantly watching your hands for some kind of deadly omen, but it is nice to be aware before you hit a bump in the road. Here are some common warning signs that may range from a red flag to keep you on your guard to a serious indication that your personal integrity is starting to get way out of line. Remember not to view these with too much anxiety. Palms can change, and these warnings may disappear with time if you change your choices in life. Similarly, they may linger on as a badge showing how you learned from a challenge in life.

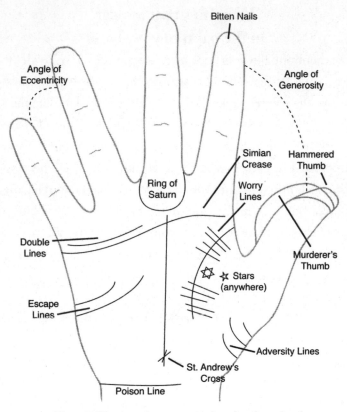

Figure 7: Warnings that appear in the palm of your hand

Adversity lines: Beginning at the thumb edge of the hand and curving upward through the mount of Venus, these lines, when present, represent an enemy or opponent. If you see one or more adversity lines appear, you are about to be challenged with conflict. Strive to make the struggle a period of growth in your life, to make you a better person. Otherwise the line will stay on your hand as the mark of a person who is against you.

Angle of eccentricity: The angle between your Apollo or ring finger and your Mercury or pinkie finger when you spread them wide is your angle of eccentricity, and everyone has one. This shows how much your personality, behavior, and life departs from the norm. It isn't automatically bad to have a large angle—in fact, my angle of eccentricity is quite large—but if you notice that it is getting larger, you may want to take a look at recent changes you've made. It is important to make sure that your behavior is still socially acceptable in most cases and that you haven't gone off the deep end.

Angle of generosity: Everyone has an angle between the thumb and Jupiter or pointer finger, but you should watch carefully for changes over time in that angle when you open your hand wide. If the angle increases dramatically, you'll have a hard time holding onto money, while if the angle shrinks substantially, you may be getting a bit stingy.

Bitten nails: Have you started (or renewed) biting your nails recently? Not only is this a common habit, and one hard to break, it also means that you are letting self-criticism get the better of you. Bitten nails are not just an obvious sign of stress. They are evidence of a deeper personality issue developing. You are letting your fears and worries take control.

Double lines: A line parallel to the life line is usually a good thing, but if you see railroad tracks appearing on other lines, especially more than one, it may mean you're beginning to lead a double life. Double lines on the heart line and life lines, for example, may warn that you need to make a choice between two lovers before you end up being one of those people with secret families in a different state.

Escape lines: Starting on the percussive edge of the hand and wrapping horizontally across the lunar mount, these lines indicate a person who tries to run away from problems either physically or with drugs and/or alcohol.

Hammered thumb: A thumb that when viewed from the side looks flattened can indicate goals being lost due to your ego's demands. If the thumb has a flattened tip as well, as if it has been stubbed, this can show that you're being manipulative instead of motivational.

Murderer's thumb: An extremely fat, thick, and wide thumb that bulges bulbously doesn't mean that you're headed for jail time, but it warns that you may have lost self-control.

Poison line: Starting on the percussive edge of the hand, very low on the lunar mount, and crossing horizontally to the mount of Venus, the presence of this line can indicate a physical constitution that is given to addictions or allergies.

Ring of Saturn: A curved line cupping your mount of Saturn below your middle finger is a sign that there is a big barrier to a goal in your life. Unless you can remove this barrier, and see the line fade as a result, you will have to change a goal entirely.

Simian crease: Do your heart and head lines seem to be moving closer together over time, perhaps even combining into a single line on one hand or the other? This new line, called the simian crease, can indicate you are becoming too single-minded or stubborn. It can also signal that a broadening of your horizons may be necessary or forced upon you in your future.

St. Andrew's cross: A cross low on the rising line of Saturn, if you have one, especially one that goes toward your lunar mount on the percussive side of your hand, traditionally has meant that you will have the opportunity to save a life. Though this is a great thing, I have placed it in the warning section so you can be vigilant and make sure you know your CPR and first aid.

Star: Yes, these were mentioned along with other warning markers, but it bears repeating that the appearance of a new pentagram or Star of David in the palm, as opposed to an asterisk, can be a serious cause for pause and reflection before proceeding. Don't freak out—just carefully note where on your hand the star has formed, and take a break or retreat from that corresponding area of life to make sure you're making the right decisions.

Worry lines: Many people have small lines radiating out from the base of the thumb across the Venus mount. Some people have very few, while others have an uncountable number. Take a look at your active or dominant hand. If you see those worry lines radiating out so far as to cross the life line, your worrying may be starting to affect your health in a way that could worsen in the future, as if you needed more to worry about.

A hand of a different color

Forget mood rings—your skin changes color on its own to reflect your emotions, wellness, and intuition. The biggest warning signs aren't little signs in the palm, but rather changes that seem to affect your whole hand. Now that you've inspected your hand carefully for red flags, take a look at the big picture and see if you can't find some gray flags or blue flags as well. Often these color changes begin as small dots, and if the warnings are not heeded, they spread into blotches and eventually your entire palm or hand can take on a different hue. Below are the meanings of some color and texture changes as well as other holistic characteristics of the hand that should not be overlooked.

White or pale coloring: This can be a sign of poor circulation, brought about by illness. Check with your doctor if this is an ongoing change in your entire hand.

Black or gray coloring: Bruising or a gray complexion is not only a potential bad health sign, but also represents depression, failure, and endings in your life.

Red: Showing an intensity and passion often associated with love or anger, a redness of the hands indicates that you are about to take a strong action that will be fulfilled to completeness.

Pink: This is a healthy sign in the palm, and indicates happiness.

Mottling: This can indicate nervousness, being of two minds on an issue, or an emotional roller coaster.

Yellow: This can be a serious indication relating to the liver's health; see your doctor.

Green: A lack of self-control and, yes, even envy, are represented by greenish tinges to the hand.

Blue: Depression, heart problems both literal and figurative, or poor circulation due to illness.

Texture: Press down on your hand with your other hand's thumb and then remove the pressure and watch for a reaction. Does a white mark linger, or does your skin spring back into shape instantly? Do this check often to notice changes in the reaction of your hand to pressure. This reflects your own ability to react to the pressures of life, so if the mark lingers or if you can make a dent in your hand that stays, you may be at the end of your rope. A fat hand with a lack of muscles shows a period of rest in your life, while if your hand is soft without extra flab, it shows a lack of energy or motivation. Elasticity of the skin is a good sign, while tough skin represents a period of hard work ahead of you. Rough or thick skin shows a focus on the self and your internal moral fiber, while thin and soft skin shows perceptiveness toward others more than the self.

Flexibility: The physical flexibility of your hand relates directly to your metaphorical flexibility to change. So if you notice that you're getting especially limber or developing a new double-jointedness, you may need some more structure in your life. If you are feeling stiff, it may be time to welcome change with open arms instead of putting up strong resistance.

Moisture: Sweaty hands represent stress and nervousness, yes, but if they are always sweaty they may indicate a person who shares too much with the world. If the clamminess is new, it might show an illness coming on.

Temperature: Cold or hot hands can be a sign of illness, and they can also signal major energy changes afoot in life, though some people always have cold hands due to circulation. I have naturally cold hands myself, but I always tend to get even more cold when in the presence of another person giving off a lot of energy, whether it be angry or healing.

Shape: The major hand types based on shape will be explored further in chapter 4. Usually, the hand shape doesn't change quickly, though you will notice a change from baby hands to adulthood. However, it is possible for your hand structure to start changing fundamentally in front of your eyes due to a combination of all of the above effects of texture, injury, weight fluctuation, and fluid content. If you see an overall big change, know that your essential nature is getting an overhaul, and make sure that the person you are is changing into the person you want to be.

Adding insult to injury

Don't ignore cuts and bruises on your hand when using palmistry as a daily guide. As mentioned earlier, deformities and birthmarks should not be shyly excluded from a palm reading, because they are a part of who you are and the plan of who you are to become. Likewise, small injuries that you make to your hand can also be a feedback loop from your own intuition creating warnings that were destined to be there. Whenever you bruise or cut your hand or even break a finger, take a look back at the regions of the hand detailed after your morning checks in order to determine what area of your life may be affected by this change to your hand. Some palmists are even especially careful of acupuncture, jewelry, tattoos, and body modifications such as implants that are located on the hand due to the effects they may have on one's destiny. Deliberate actions to change your destiny will be explored later in this book. For now, here are a few accidental hand changes and what they might mean.

Breaks: A broken bone is a big deal in the hand, as it can require physical therapy to be fully functional again. Likewise, the palmistry meaning of a break can mean a major internal personality overhaul is taking place that will take time and significant energy to get through. For example, a broken pinkie finger may mean that you are trying to become a more honest communicator, but that it will take time and effort to build trust with people to whom you have lied in the past.

Burns: Fire represents transformation, and a burn to the hand means that something can't continue on the way it was. Not only has the area of your life been destroyed, but the hope of new beginnings and creations has replaced what once was, like a phoenix rising from the ashes. For example, a burn to the heart line can mean that a relationship with a lover is being destroyed in order to make room for a new love in your life.

Bruises: A bruise represents a dark time in your life that requires retreat in order to heal and move forward. For example, a bruise to your Venus mount at the base of your thumb may represent depression over the loss of a lover. The advice is to take time by yourself to return to your former independent glory rather than jumping straight into a rebound relationship with someone new.

Cuts: No matter how accidental a cut may be, when interpreting a cut as a palmistry sign, think about the deliberate actions you may be making in your life to end things or part ways with something or someone you once knew. For example, a slip of the knife that cuts your middle finger may mean that you are subconsciously sabotaging your work life, perhaps by picking a fight with your boss that could end with you getting fired or looking for work elsewhere. A tiny cut means a small ending, while a cut requiring stitches means you may have other major repairs to do elsewhere in your life.

Punctures: An accidental jab with a nail can mean more than just a need for a tetanus shot. Puncture wounds tend to represent an increased flow of energy in that area of your life, so you'll need to assess what area of your life is getting more energy and find a productive way to use it so that it doesn't bleed you dry. For example, a poked pointer finger can mean that you need to do something in your life in a leadership role. Maybe it's time to lead a scouting troop or get a new job as an administrator so you won't turn into a bossy tyrant in your home or love life.

Scars: Even after scars have healed, they can change, fade, or rise up and become keloid over time. Interpret a scar as a badge of honor from the meaning of the original injury, but watch it carefully for how that influence still affects you. For example, a puncture under the middle finger might represent a falling out with an estranged father figure, and the scar becoming more prominent over time may indicate how the past is affecting your relationships with men.

Scrapes: A scrape represents a close call or a brush with danger that should warn you to go back to basics and build your foundations. For example, a scrape to your destiny line in the center of your palm coming down from your middle finger may mean that you narrowly avoided losing a large amount of money, and that you should make sure you have insurance policies paid in full and an adequate nest egg saved up in case of emergencies.

Experimentation and reflection to create change

In the previous chapter, we explored different ways to systematically document changes in your hands as well as things you should see when you try to change your destiny after observing signs in the palm of your hand. Naturally, the process of experimentation and reflection will be put into play when you work on this practice. For example, you will see a red dot appear on your heart line, work to cool feelings of anger and resentment toward your spouse through meditation and communication, and then look back at your palm to reflect on how well it worked. Has the red dot vanished along with those negative feelings? Great job! Record your success in your palmistry journal. Is the red dot still there, accompanied by your frustration? Experiment again, perhaps with couples counseling, to find other ways to solve the problem. The cycle of experimentation and reflection is important, because without one or the other, the process of changing your destiny using palmistry is impossible.

In the above example, it is easy to see how not changing actions or not carefully reviewing how those actions helped your life can make the practice impossible. However, you must be even more mindful if you are trying to create a positive sign in your life and in your palm, rather than simply heeding a warning sign.

I'll be the first to admit that waiting for a sign to appear is about as exciting as watching paint dry. If you see a warning sign, it is easier to anxiously spot check to make sure it is disappearing. Spending the same energy watching for a positive sign to appear, however, can be an exercise in frustration. Repeating experiments is harder when you see nothing because it's possible to feel your experiments will never work, even if you are right on the verge of a discovery.

The key to successfully seeing the results of a positive change in your palm and your life is to simply not give up. Try not to get obsessive about it, and set a reasonable schedule for change. Keep updating your palmistry journal on a monthly basis and set goals for yourself within that time frame (or longer if practical) so you won't give up after a few days. Some helpful examples of how to track your goals in specific areas of your life or personal characteristics will be carefully explored in the following chapters. For now, we'll take a look at how to make some of those positive signs appear in the palms of your hands.

Pink dots

Pink dots are positive signs that are based on general good health. A pink dot can mean that you have the potential for a joyful day full of success and making new friends. You can start to generate more pink dots through regular exercise, a nutritious diet, and by following your doctor's advice. Think of those pink dots as little batteries that can help you find energy and power even when your emotional and spiritual energy may seem to be running low. They can appear within minutes of initiating healthy activities for your physical wellness.

Squares

Squares in the palm are signs of stability and strength, a well of energy that can last for a long time. In order to bring more stability to your life, you'll have to work on your foundations such as setting up a savings account at the bank, scheduling a date night with your spouse to keep romance and friendship alive, or spring cleaning and maintaining your house in order to nurture a comfortable home. You may see new squares slowly appear over the course of a month or more, or you may see existing squares deepen and become more noticeable.

Ovals

Ovals are a feminine symbol, and they represent gifts or making an ally. If you believe in goddess spirituality, prayers and worship to female deities can make ovals appear or deepen. If you are female or just want to get in touch with your feminine side, working on your passive and receptive qualities can help. Just being thankful can make gifts and ovals appear in your life. Taking active steps to befriend women or to show your allegiance to a female authority figure can also deepen or manifest ovals over the course of a month or more.

Circles

Like the square, you can think of a circle as a well of energy. Circles are usually associated with solving a specific problem by adapting or changing yourself rather than just struggling through the issue without modifying your plans or attitude. Work on flexibility in your life, including your scheduling, compromises with others, and even your personal goals. Once you begin to adapt to a problem at hand, you may find new circles forming or existing circles becoming more prominent.

Triangles

Triangles are also wells of energy, like circles or squares, but they often represent smashing through a problem or transcending and avoiding it entirely. Try to make choices and move forward without looking back, as fence-sitting and hesitation are a surefire way to let triangles fade. Working on your assertiveness by clearly communicating your needs and desires as well as taking small but measurable steps toward your goal can make triangles appear or deepen.

Crosses

Crosses are a great sign that energy is focusing on an area of your life like a laser beam. It is the nature of focus to only happen in one place at a time, so if you are hoping for a cross to appear, you'll have to make a firm decision about where your priorities lie. Then, simplify your life so that you are more clearly spending your time and energy on what you value instead of wasting your efforts and spreading yourself too thin. You should see a cross begin to appear in a domain when the time is right to take the next step in that area of your life. Chapter 4 has more information on focusing on a specific area of your life.

Deepening, lengthening, branching, and doubling lines

As I wrote before, you can imagine the analogy of rivers to understand how the depths of your lines represent your spiritual and life energy flow. In general, deep lines, doubled lines, long lines, and those that are branching are what you want. However, you also want to seek balance so that one line isn't flooding with all the energy while the other areas of your hand and your life are experiencing a drought. Thus, while it is important to choose areas of focus—and there will be more about those in later chapters—please don't do so to the exclusion of all other areas of your life.

So how do you increase energy in an area of your life? Turn your thoughts to that area of your life more often, and put effort into that area in order to remove blockages and increase energy flow. For example, if you want to deepen your heart line, you can think about your lover or the best traits of a potential lover. Pray about your ideal love life, journal about the feelings in your heart, and take classes or read books on relationships.

Major line changes take a long time to form. Although thin branches can appear over a month's time, true deepening and lengthening can take years to form, and some people just naturally have shallow and chaining lines. Shallow and chaining lines that last a lifetime don't mean that you don't have enough energy for what you need. Instead, think of yourself as a more efficient engine that requires less fuel than most people to get the same amount of things done.

Smoothing or toughening your skin

Ideally, most people want to be perceptive and observant while still being tough enough to withstand the slings and arrows of interactions with others and disappointments in life. If you are too thin-skinned, you may be far too sensitive, and your empathy can become disabling. If you are too thick-skinned, others may think that you are unfeeling or cruel, and you may not be able to experience deep spiritual joy and love.

If you think your skin is too thick and rough, the right moisturizer won't fix the palmistry meaning of that insensitivity. Work to open yourself up through artistic pursuits, emotional communication with others, and allowing yourself to be vulnerable to people you love and trust. On the other hand, if you find yourself to be too thin-skinned, practice finding your inner spiritual reserves through prayer, meditation, exercise, nutrition, and working on your assertiveness and healthy boundaries. The texture of your skin can change quite rapidly, even overnight, in response to lifestyle modifications.

Working on your flexibility

Earlier in the section on warning signs (p. 49), I went over how to change your angle of generosity or your angle of eccentricity if either was becoming too stiff or too loose. In general, though, greater flexibility in your hand represents a better resilience and willingness to adapt to change in your life. If you have stiff hands and are rigid and inflexible in your ways of thinking, take small steps toward change. Of course, if you have arthritis or are differently abled, your hands may never be fully flexible, which doesn't mean you'll always be a stick in the mud—everything is relative. Watch for changes in your flexibility, rather than comparing your flexibility to others. If you want to increase your flexibility, work on compromising with people around you, changing your schedule, mixing up your scenery with travel, and stepping outside of your comfort zone by trying new things. You should notice your hand flexibility change over the course of weeks or months of gently stretching yourself, metaphorically that is.

Camera's eye

If you want a job as a photographer, a graphic designer, or in any field that requires a sharp eye for detail and a sense of something being wrong or right with all things visual like an air traffic controller, the mark of the camera's eye is a good sign to see. In fact, the more important it is to you to see these perfect pictures, the longer and deeper you should hope to develop that line rising up under your ring finger. Keen observation does require skill, so if you have no rising line under your ring finger you'll have to work on building that skill. I suggest you start by working through the section on developing personality traits, in chapter 4. If you already have some aptitude, keep your skills sharp through frequent practice of observation. This can be done at your job, in a journal or sketchbook, or by playing games that hone your senses. You should see a camera's eye lengthen or deepen over a month or more, but to make one appear where none existed before may take years of effort.

Girdle of Venus

The horizontal line cupping your middle and ring fingers is a good sign to develop and to look for if you are trying to spice up a romance that is beginning to wane over time, like a passionate marriage gone stale, or if the sensual joys are something you are trying to bring back into your life in a positive way. For example, if you have not yet had sex, or are hoping to renew your sexuality after the death of a lover or a traumatic sexual experience, nurturing and waiting for a strong girdle of Venus can be one way to decide when you are ready.

Since the sensuality of the girdle of Venus does not only pertain to sex, you can begin to strengthen or form one by learning to appreciate the finer things in life (such as art) and other things pertaining to beautiful aesthetics. Activities could include the pleasures of gourmet food, walks in beautiful surroundings, bubble baths, and massage. Pamper yourself and work on getting in touch with pure joy and pleasure by understanding your deepest needs and desires so you can communicate them to a lover. A girdle of Venus can take a month or more to deepen, but may take much longer to newly form where one did not appear previously, so be patient with yourself.

Hourglass on your mount of Jupiter

These two triangles forming under your pointer finger are often thought of as marks of karma or payback for good that has been given to others. Since the hourglass on the mount of Jupiter represents the establishment of a mutually beneficial relationship, it is an excellent sign to watch for before entering into a business partnership, attempting to negotiate a new child custody agreement, or introducing a serious significant other to your family. Since the essential spiritual nature of the hourglass under Jupiter is good karma, start by giving the energy into the universe that you want to receive without expecting immediate returns. The more you target the people with which you wish to establish a beneficial relationship the better, but even volunteer work and charity giving can strengthen the energy of the hourglass or make the hourglass bigger.

Since the mark of the hourglass under Jupiter represents selfless giving and open receiving from the universe as a result, expect that this mark may take longer to achieve than others if you have a specific goal in mind that may hamper the selfless aspect of your giving or set you back by making you feel resentful if you don't immediately get blessings in return. Although it would be possible to see the hourglass under Jupiter in a month's time, this mark can be a spiritual journey that takes a lifetime to achieve.

Mark of the teacher

There are many ways to be a teacher, so the mark of the teacher is what I believe to be one of the more easy signs to see form in your hand if you don't yet have one. Before taking on the tough job of becoming a school teacher or working with disadvantaged youth, it would be a good idea to wait for a sign that you are right for the job, and the mark of the teacher would be a good indicator. These two diagonal lines under your pinkie finger (one is between the head and heart lines) can be accentuated by many small vertical lines under your pinkie finger if you are a teacher of children. In fact, as teachers gain experience and skill, these little vertical lines can become quite numerous, like little tally marks of success. Sometimes the person is such a good teacher that it is hard to discern the difference in the palm between his or her own children and the many pupils that have been helped to succeed. More about family planning can be read in chapter 5.

To darken or multiply lines that indicate pupils or marks of the teacher, you can simply find ways to take on the role of passing on knowledge and understanding in your life. That can mean volunteering, working on creating traditions and closeness with your own children, helping someone to initiate a spiritual practice, or training others in a skill. Do this and you can find those changes in the palm of your hand in a month or more. If you have neither marks of the teacher nor pupils indicated yet, read ahead to the section on working on your personality traits and focus on your communication skills. These teaching marks can appear after a year or more of effort.

Medical stigmata

These five parallel lines on the mount underneath your pinkie finger have to do with the work of a healer, but there are many ways to bring healing into the lives of others. If you plan to dedicate your life to healing people or animals—whether the healing be physical, emotional, or spiritual—waiting for medical stigmata can be a good sign before dropping a lot of money on medical school or quitting your job to join a healing monastery.

To deepen or lengthen medical stigmata that you already have, you can focus on multiplying the number of people that you already help in a healing way. Even if you are not a doctor or a nurse, perhaps you offer emotional healing for your loved ones in times of need, or tend to your family when they are sick or injured. The key to medical stigmata is to keep your skills sharp through frequent practice.

If you have no medical stigmata at all, think about ways that you can gain healing skills, such as taking a massage, first aid, or CPR class; learning mediation skills to heal the emotional rifts of those who are in conflict; or learning a spiritual healing discipline such as Reiki or prayer. Remember to take care of yourself first. If you seek to heal others without first mastering your own physical, emotional, and spiritual wellness, you may not be successful. Because of the difficulty of maintaining your own health while becoming a healer, acquiring medical stigmata can take a lifetime to attain.

Mystic cross or cross of mystery

This cross under the middle finger, or under the junction of your middle and ring fingers, is a sign of a proclivity for the occult. The mystic cross is a good omen to see before beginning a serious path of study into magic, such as accepting initiation into Wicca or ceremonial magic. Because it is the cross of mystery, the ways of obtaining this mark can be confusing, mysterious, and different for each individual.

If you want to deepen or enlarge a mystic cross, increasing your discipline in daily occult practice such as devotional rituals or meditation can do the trick. The mystic cross can take years to make an observable change. If you have no cross of mystery at all, one may be difficult or impossible to obtain, since serious study in the occult may not be everyone's cup of tea. You can begin working on your mystic cross by getting to know yourself as a spiritual person, researching occult practices, and determining which path of study you wish to take. Forming a mystic cross can take a lifetime, or not occur at all. Absence of a mystic cross doesn't mean you can't perform magic or worship as a Pagan, just that occult work may not be your essential vocation in life.

Relocation lines

Relocation lines are usually thin lines that branch out from your life line in all directions. The funny thing about relocation lines is that they often appear when the option to move or do some serious travel crops up in your mind as a conscious or subconscious choice, rather than appearing before any move as a warning. If you want to relocate, it isn't necessary to just sit around and wait for relocation lines to appear in your palm. That said, those lines can help you evaluate your choices once you start processing big decisions.

For example, if you want desperately to get out of where you're living (no matter where to) and there are no relocation lines to be seen in your palm, don't fret. Start by making some plans for several potential options. Make arbitrary choices if you need to, but apply for jobs and price out homes in practical locations. Within weeks of making plans to move, you may notice thin lines branching away from your life line. These are your potential relocations. Longer lines represent location options that are farther away, while short branches may be in your current neighborhood. Lines lower on the life line show that the potential move would need a lot more time to make happen, while lines higher up mean that a quick move is within your reach. Observing carefully to see which lines appear first, deepest, and highest up on the life line can help you make your choice. Relocation lines might stay on your hand for life, even after you make your move.

Sister line

Double lines parallel to one another are usually a good sign, if you aren't spreading yourself too thin or leading a secret double life as a result. They usually just represent extra sources of strength, energy, and fulfillment. Developing a sister line to your life line is the best, since that adds to your health and abundance of life energy.

Developing a double line means taking care of yourself to increase energy, just like in the instructions on deepening and lengthening your existing lines. Making a sister line can be tricky, because you should carefully add a fulfilling role to your life without losing your life balance. For example, one woman might choose to be a wife and a mother and an employee. Those roles can fulfill her and feed into each other to make her feel like a complete human being. Such a woman may have deep but balanced lines that include a sister line to her life line. Another woman may choose to be a wife and mother but feel overwhelmed by those roles. Perhaps this individual would prefer to work outside the home and is a frustrated stay-at-home mom and resentful wife as a result. Such a woman may have some deep lines representing her attempts to focus on family, but overall the lines on her palm may be shallow and chained, and if she has a sister line to her life line at all, it is faint. Perhaps choosing to be an employee would help balance the second woman's lines and deepen the sister line she has already.

Choosing to carefully balance fulfilling life roles can help deepen and maintain a sister line over the years. If you have no sister line at all, you can choose to wear other hats in your life that may be enough to boost your energy and ambition without making you lose focus on the identity you already have. Perhaps volunteering for a role in an organization, strengthening your cultural identity, or deepening your spiritual practice will be enough to form a sister line. Sister lines always take a long time—sometimes years—to form, if at all. Remember that while some people seem to run on more efficient or different energy levels, and won't be able to form sister lines, they are definitely not deficient or lacking in any way.

Star on Apollo

A star on a rising line of Apollo or on the mount under the ring finger can occasionally be a bad thing if you're not the type of person who likes to call attention to yourself. However, it is a wonderful sign to see if you are hoping to audition as an actor, model, or dancer. It could go either way to see a star on Apollo before becoming a politician, since it can be an omen that you will become famous or infamous. If you are ready for the drama that can come into your life from becoming the center of attention for your own creative efforts, it could be time to work on earning that star, but be aware that it will shake up your life.

Although working on your artistic talent can be a wonderful way to build a foundation for a positive experience of fame and a star of Apollo, the next step is essential. One must gain public exposure and notoriety for one's creative expression, which can be positive or negative. Strive to put forth the image you choose to project. A star of Apollo can appear before a press release or a media interview, when word of mouth travels organically, or if something on the Internet goes viral.

The star of Apollo is made out of lines and is thus not extremely fast forming. Though an existing star can seem to deepen quickly (like within a month or more), forming a star of Apollo can happen slowly, years before the fame or notoriety destined to follow.

Triangle of earnings

The triangle of earnings is formed by the head line (the middle of the three horizontal lines on your hand), the destiny line (vertical line to your middle finger), and the rising line of Mercury (the diagonal line to your pinkie finger. Ideally, you want the triangle to be closed—to earn and hold on to money. The bigger the triangle, the larger the amount of money, so unless you want otherwise, bigger is better. Looking at the potential issues with your triangle is necessary when watching for a sign from your triangle of earnings.

Are you missing a destiny line rising up to your middle finger, or does that line have an opening in your triangle? That means you have to work on job stability, creating savings, and other financial responsibilities. Basically, think of this line as representing all of those boring obligations that are necessary for creating long-term foundations. This line may be a tough one to work on if you are the type of person who, like me, enjoys hopping from one project to the next and thinking up new and exciting business ideas.

Are you missing a rising line to Mercury, or is there a gap in your triangle on that line going up to your pinkie finger? That means you have some wheeling and dealing to do. Making business deals, the right transactions, the right connections with people, and using your words and winning ways to earn raises and promotions is the name of the game with this important line. Whereas destiny line work may frustrate people who love wild schemes, working on the rising line to Mercury may be uncomfortable for those who don't want to rock the boat.

Is there a gap or an opening in your triangle on the edge or corners where it should be completed by the head line? This warning sign means that your thinking about money is perhaps misinformed, and the way you budget or spend your money could be causing some big problems. Find a trusted financial planner to be your guide, and consider some books and/or classes on saving and spending money wisely. A slight shift in your priorities or your perceptions surrounding your finances may be all that's needed, but pushing back against a lifetime of thinking a certain way is never easy.

After you seal up your triangle of earnings, the next step to improve your financial outlook is to make the triangle bigger. By reading the earlier descriptions in this chapter, you may already know that one side of your triangle may need more work than the others; ideally you should have harmonious growth in all aspects of your triangle of earnings. Financial planners use the analogy of a three-legged table supported by saving, reducing debt, and earning. If any of those legs aren't there or of equal length, the table will not stand. Likewise, you shouldn't build up one side of your triangle to the exclusion of all others.

To move your destiny line away from the center of your palm to enlarge your triangle of earnings, work on the practical more than the creative, and align yourself with the right authority figures and leadership roles. To move your Mercury line away from the center of your palm, increase your communication and business skills to make sure that you're networking with the right people. To move your head line away from the center of your palm to enlarge your triangle of earnings, make sure that you are doing what you love and that you love what you do, so that your heart and your work to earn a living are in harmony. Try to take baby steps toward each of the above goals at the same time so you can slowly improve each area of life in a balanced way.

As with other lines, deepening triangle of earnings lines or lengthening them to fill up gaps can take a month or more, and making lines emerge where they do not exist can take a lifetime. Enlarging your triangle of earnings should also be understood as a lifelong challenge, so keep your observations over years rather than checking every day.

Via lascivia

Like the girdle of Venus, this horizontal line curving from around the pointer finger and middle finger junction to the ring finger (or, the junction between your ring finger and pinkie finger) has to do with sensuality and passion. Unlike the girdle of Venus, however, this line is more focused on physical pleasure than all the other good things in life. To have a great marriage or love partnership, it is good to see the girdle of Venus at least, and better to have both the girdle of Venus and via lascivia. The via lascivia alone won't make a relationship unless passion and sex are the only things you're looking for. If you are looking for a no-strings-attached fling or needing only to improve your sex life, the via lascivia is a good line to watch.

To lengthen or deepen an existing via lascivia, getting to know your own body in a sensual way is an excellent place to start. If you have no via lascivia at all and have noticed a lack of libido and enjoyment of sensual pleasures, dig deeper to find the cause of your issues with eroticism. Perhaps your attitude about sex is blocking your progression as a sexual being; a medical problem may be a physical barrier; or maybe a traumatic physical violation must be addressed carefully through therapy.

Though deepening or lengthening a via lascivia can take a month or more, forming the via lascivia can be a life's work. Don't fret if you don't have one at all and can't seem to form one. Not everyone is unhappy without a via lascivia, and it doesn't mean that you are frigid or unattractive. Some people find the source of their arousal and sexual pleasure in mental stimulation with a partner or in a deep romantic connection, producing lines connecting the heart line with the head line or rising line to Mercury instead of a via lascivia.

So far, we've looked at examples of positive signs that can bring joy to your life. However, don't be disappointed if you can't seem to force them to appear by experimenting with simple changes. If you're lucky enough to earn a mark of a teacher by volunteering at a preschool or to expand your triangle of earnings with some careful investments, it could be that you were naturally predisposed to those blessings. If, like most of us, you strive for things that don't always come easily, you may have to go back to basics—do some groundwork on your most ingrained character traits before your actions bring about the change you desire. If you find yourself giving up on a positive sign, read ahead to the chapter on performing specific readings to work with your personality traits to find out if there's something you can do systematically to better play to your strengths. There's also something to be said for waiting for the right time for growth in your life. If focusing on one change isn't doing it for you right now, try shifting your attention to something else to build your confidence before trying again.

What can a person do with these changes?

We'll go over how to change your ways when you see basic personality traits that you don't like in your fingers or on the lines of your hands in the chapter about performing specific readings. However, since we've already gone over many warning signs and red flags in this book, I'd like to take some time to go over what you should do when you see those warning signs, and what you might see in your hand as a result.

Black, blue, red, yellow, or white dots

Colored dots usually appear quickly and can disappear just as quickly. Take care to note the location of the dot, as it can hold a clue about what area of your life needs work. For example, a black dot on the heart line might indicate depression over a love life quandary, while a similar dot on the

destiny line could indicate depression over being impover-
ished financially. Those black dots of depression should be
taken seriously with actions taken to alleviate your emotional pain. If you've had that dot and associated sadness or
hopelessness for a while, counseling or medical treatment
for mental illness could be indicated. Blue dots are usually
more transient and less severe, but if they last for over three
months, the depression can be considered equivalent. A red
dot doesn't have to be a bad thing, but that mark of passionate energy should remind you to cool your anger or lust
before it gets you into trouble. Yellow dots are a warning
to visit your doctor for a checkup; white dots can mean a
health issue too, or they can indicate that your energy is too
diffuse and scattered, so you should bring more focus to the
area of your life indicated by the dot. Once you correct the
problem associated with the dots in your palmistry reading,
you should see them disappear entirely.

Stars, tridents, grids, or grilles

These tiny lines can appear slowly or quickly, or they may
stick with you for life, growing more or less noticeable as
a warning sign to you. Stars are usually major signs asking
you to retreat or withdraw within yourself. Maybe you need
a spiritual vacation, a break from a relationship, or a day off
of work. Think of tridents like forks in the road. Tridents
encourage you to slow down and come to a complete decision before proceeding ahead at your normal speed. Grids
and grilles are both obstacles, so you may have to choose

another path entirely or break through that obstacle before moving forward in your life. Once these signs are dealt with, they may fade so as to become unnoticeable (unless you get out your magnifying glass), disappear entirely, or remain on your hand as a badge of honor.

Shallow or chaining lines

Some people seem to have chaining or shallow lines on their hands for their entire lives, and so the changes may be more subtle. For others, lines becoming more shallow or chaining may be a noticeable change. Imagine that those channels in your hand are rivers of energy, and when you see the lines become shallow or chained, those rivers are drying up. A lack of energy can be a serious problem caused by illness, anxieties and fears, or too much effort being placed in one area of life that takes away from your overall balance. Observe which lines have reduced energy and whether any others are taking on more of the flow. See if you can even things out by spending more time and effort in a neglected area of your life. For example, if your life line and heart line are suddenly light and chaining while your destiny line deepens or remains the same, it may mean that you are focusing too hard on your career and need to set aside time on your calendar for regular exercise and reconnecting with your loved ones. You should see the depth of your lines even out somewhat if the change has been sudden, but don't be worried if you can't change chaining that has been in your palm your entire life. Some people just "run cool," on a lower supply of energy than other people.

Puffy, sweaty, cold, gray, or bruised hands

A change in the color or feel of your hands as a whole almost always indicates a health issue that should be inves-
tigated with a doctor as well as evaluated for emotional
components. Edema, bruising easily, and poor circulation
are all symptoms of numerous serious diseases and require
someone qualified to make a proper diagnosis. If you notice
any of these signs suddenly cropping up in your life, make
an appointment with your doctor first, and then think about
what sort of emotional stresses may be affecting your resil-
iency. Have you been suffering from a sadness that doesn't
seem to lift? Are you tired and hopeless most of the time?
Do you find yourself sharing too much or too little with
others in your life? In addition to your physical state, share
this information with your doctor, as these kinds of be-
haviors can be symptomatic of physical or mental illnesses
that are quite treatable with diet changes, exercise, or medication.

Angle of eccentricity

Do you notice a sudden extra flexibility of your pinkie finger
away from your hand, or does that finger now seem stiffer
than usual, hugging closely to your hand? A change in your
angle of eccentricity has to do with how you are conforming
to others, and it can shift throughout your life if you don't
have a hand deformity or an issue such as arthritis that pre-
vents change. If you find your pinkie finger less flexible with
regard to your hand, consider whether you are going against

your true values or nature to please someone else. For example, a gay or lesbian person who is in the closet might notice a severely decreased angle of eccentricity. At the other extreme, if you find sudden increased flexibility in this angle of eccentricity, check yourself with a trusted friend or family member to make sure you haven't gone off the deep end. The way you dress yourself, spend money, abuse substances, or talk to others may cause you to lose friends or a job. After making the necessary changes in your life associated with your angle of eccentricity, you should observe your flexibility returning to normal over time.

Angle of generosity

Like the angle of eccentricity, barring deformity or arthritis, the flexibility of your thumb away from your hand can change over your lifetime and can shift back and forth between a degree of stiffness and near double-jointedness. If your thumb hugs up close to your pointer finger, you may be too stingy, and have to find ways to release your grasp on possessions, money, or simply time and effort to become more generous. At the other extreme, if you suddenly are able to stretch your thumb far away from the rest of your hand, others could be taking advantage of you. Focus on setting healthy boundaries so you are not letting all your money, resources, and energy slip through your fingers into someone else's grasp. Even if it is a child, an elder who needs more care than you can provide, or a loved one with a substance abuse issue, consider how you can stop enabling another person. This person needs you to take care of yourself first. Over time, you should find that your angle of generosity returns to normal after making the necessary life choices.

Double lines

In general, double lines are good things, especially on the life line. Their appearance marks a good time to pause and make sure you're living the life you want. Forming on the life line, a double line is a cause for celebration: you have extra energy for whatever you want, so make sure you are putting it to good use. Any double line, especially if appearing on more than one line or on the heart line, is cause for you to consider the roles you play in your life. Are you wearing too many hats, or on the contrary, do you thrive on a busy schedule and plenty of responsibility? Do you have to make a choice between two incompatible lifestyles or lovers? It is hard to prescribe action to take when a person sees a double line, because the integrity of the situation depends on an individual's personality and values. While certainly cause for deep consideration, a double line doesn't need to be erased. However, if you find yourself simplifying your life significantly, it is possible for a second line to fade or disappear over time.

Hammered thumb

The pudginess of your thumb can change quickly—and go back to normal just as easily. A hammered thumb, or one that looks flattened or deflated when viewed from the side, is evidence of an inflated ego. Watch out, because the sudden appearance of a hammered thumb may mean that you are about to lose something precious to you because of your own swollen sense of self. For example, you may be about to lose a lover due to selfishness, or miss out on a terrific job opportunity due to pride. If you notice that the tip of the thumb is flattened when viewed from the side, this can be evidence that you are being more manipulative than you mean to be. Consider whether you are putting too much pressure on a child, lover, or subordinate, and decide how you can offer others more freedom of choice. You should notice that your thumb rounds out and seems to spring up with new life relatively quickly when you change your controlling or egomaniacal actions.

Murderer's thumb

The murderer's thumb is not the opposite of the hammered thumb, because unlike the thinning and fleshing out of the thumb that happens naturally as you gain weight or your hydration changes, the extreme fleshiness of the murderer's thumb is usually a lifelong trait. If you don't have a murderer's thumb already, you won't develop it over your lifetime. If you do have one, you're stuck with it. But a murderer's thumb doesn't mean that you're destined to rob banks or kill anyone. You'll just need to mitigate the willful personality traits associated with your murderer's thumb, just like everybody has to manage their own unique quirks. However, the degree to which your thumb may look large and fleshy can change as you struggle with the problems of willpower and self-control indicated by this character challenge. If you notice your thumb becoming more pronounced and raised, it can indicate an immediate need for control and discipline in your life, at which point you should notice your thumb returning to normal, even if "normal" is a bit larger than average.

Simian crease

A simian crease is usually something a person has over a lifetime, representing a struggle with single-mindedness. So don't be upset if you can't seem to get your head and heart lines to separate. In general, though, the head and heart lines can appear to move closer together or farther apart, even if they are not completely conjoined at a simian crease, where your focus becomes self-destructive in its singularity. You may also notice rising or descending lines connecting the two of them. Make sure that you find some balance in your life and that you are not neglecting your duties because of a lover or a mental obsession. Once you have found more harmony and peace, you may find your head and heart line move a bit farther apart from one another, connecting lines may fade, or if you have a true simian crease, you may find more lines departing away from the crease, reflecting your new pursuits and bringing balance to your palm landscape as a whole.

St. Andrew's cross

Near the bottom of the destiny line, this cross sounds like a great thing because it represents a chance for you to save a life. However, your St. Andrew's cross doesn't necessarily mean that you will be successful in your life-saving attempt, and it can be quite traumatic to witness a preventable death, especially that of a loved one. For that reason, a St. Andrew's cross should be a taken as a blessing, but also a cause for concern. Take a course on first aid and CPR training to make sure you are up to date on the latest lifesaving techniques. If you live near a body of water or a pool, a lifesaving course and rescue supplies could be helpful in the event of a water rescue. If you work as a doctor, nurse, EMT, firefighter, police officer, or a similar occupation, reviewing safety protocol and making sure you always have backup safety checks in place are indicated. Double check that your smoke detectors, car safety restraints, fire extinguishers, first aid kit, and disaster supplies are all in top condition. After the life is saved or lost, some people notice the St. Andrew's cross fades a bit, but others wear it for a lifetime as a reminder of their time of courage in crisis, no matter what the outcome.

Yellowed or bitten nails

Yellowed nails can represent a health problem that warrants a trip to the doctor, while bitten nails represent fears and anxieties taking control of your life. In the case of bitten nails, palmistry practitioners experience a kind of origin paradox. If one stops biting one's nails, will the fears and anxieties disappear? Or, if the fears and anxieties are eliminated, will the nail-biting habit cease entirely? The issue is a bit like the debate between genetics and environment on how a person grows up. Since we can't raise a child without an environment or without genetics, it is impossible to say that a trait is completely one or the other. Both nature and nurture work in concert to make us who we are, and likewise, our physical traits on our hands are a reflection of our choices as well as our potential and limitations. Just as you could choose to lose weight by starving yourself, you could try to change your destiny by painting your nails with foul substances so that you won't bite them, but without a lifestyle overhaul, neither will result in the change of mindset that you truly need. It is best to attack both issues in tandem, working emotionally with your anxieties through exercise and therapy or medication if necessary, and externally on the nail-biting habit by reminding yourself to stop. Though tackling a lifetime of bad habits and natural proclivities is easier said than done, your success will be evidenced by healthier nails and a more relaxed demeanor.

Injuries

The same origin paradox of bitten nails applies to the philosophy behind interpreting injuries in palmistry. If you had never hurt your hand in such a way, would you never have had the resulting understanding of your life? Likewise, if one were to deliberately injure himself or herself, could destiny be changed as a result? Palmistry is not as simplistic as this faulty logic would suggest. Water is wet and dolphins are wet, but we do not drink dolphins. Likewise, causing an injury to your palm does not automatically cause your life to change, even if injuries are a result of life changes.

Though it is true we are looking at cause and effect, remember that you are looking at a natural reflection of yourself, as if you were gazing into the image of your face in a lake. If you deliberately splash the water so that your image is distorted, you do not perceive your face in the most accurate way, regardless of whether the splashing was done in anger or by accident. Instead of making the mistake of ascribing too much power to the lines of your hands (as opposed to the actions your hands take), think of injuries to your hands as additional spiritual interpretations to add to the understanding you would gain from any close call.

For example, let's imagine a different close call. Imagine you are driving down the street, drowsy after a sleepless night. Nodding off, you roll into a tree and come out of your car with a few bumps and bruises, shaky but relatively unharmed. Naturally, you will decide to never drive drowsy again, preferring to stop at a rest area to nap or leaving home in the first place only when you are rested. Using a palmistry reading to interpret your state of mind should be done with the intent to understand the underlying cause of the accident, just as you understood that it was the drowsiness and not simply the act of driving you should avoid forever. The location of injuries on the hand will help you to tease out the differences between cause and motivation when looking at an effect, which will help you to discover the spiritual meaning behind the injury.

Four

HOW TO DO
SPECIFIC READINGS

If you're new to palmistry, by now you may be feeling pretty overwhelmed by the enormous wealth of information in the palms of your hands. There are so many lines, bumps, and blotches, and they're all seemingly the same! How can the average person remember them all, much less watch for tiny changes? As a professional palm reader, I will admit to using palmistry to the very limit of its awesome potential. But anyone can use palmistry changes in a practical way; the trick is to narrow your focus.

For example, keeping track of a street map's road changes due to construction and traffic every day would be maddening if you tried to keep on top of an entire city's busy details. However, if you just glance at a website, watch the news, or consult a GPS display of your route to work, you can easily see if construction or a bad accident has messed up your commute so you can take a simple detour. Likewise, if your main focus in life is, say, finding a job or a girlfriend, you don't have to spend all your palm-reading time looking deeply into what pets might be best for you. You can always come to me for a professional and in-depth reading for plenty of details.

Watching a specific aspect of your palm for change

So far in this book we've taken a look at each the palm or hand as a whole, and also scanned specific regions for warning signs, good omens, and broad trends. In this chapter, I'll show you a different technique for focusing on one topic instead of one type of sign or region of your hand. These two techniques can be used simultaneously or separately depending on your need. I suggest you keep up with the morning and night checks with your journal on a daily basis so you can practice and keep the different meanings fresh in your mind. However, if you have a specific topic of focus or situation you want to investigate in your palm, open up to a fresh page in your journal and start tracking that focus independently from your other palmistry work.

Narrowing your focus

As a professional palm reader, I find that most people don't actually want an entire rundown of their life. Rather, most of the clients I help have a specific issue at hand (no pun intended) they want looked into, whether it be a long and sordid story worthy of a daytime soap opera, or a simple question based on a major goal or life change happening at the time I read their palm. In this chapter, I will go over the most popular topics I am asked about, one by one, so you can practice focusing on just one area at a time. You don't have to make a journal entry for every single one to learn this technique. Start out by choosing the focus that is most important to you, and draw just those features in your palmistry journal. If you don't have any big life issues right now and don't feel like you need a focus, you can easily leave this chapter for a time when a big problem or issue comes up for you.

Love

The number one reason clients come to me for a palmistry reading is to figure out the direction their love lives are headed and how to make their true desires happen in the love department. I will start by directing your attention just to the parts of your palm reading that have to do with love so you can narrow your attention to just those details, and follow up by giving a few specific examples of what to look for when answering some common questions about love. Since how your love life will go depends on your lover (if you have one, or have somebody in mind), read the chapter on reading the palms of others as well, so you can do some important comparisons to see if you've found your match.

For now, let's look at your love destiny as reflected in your own hands, starting with a map of both your dominant and passive hands. So get out your palmistry journal and just draw the features of your hand that have to do with love, omitting other details as if they weren't even there. We'll start building a map of your love life from the ground up.

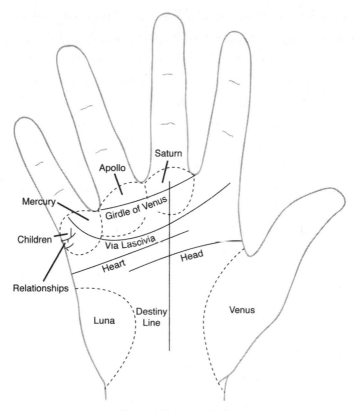

Figure 8: Palmistry for love

Climbing mountains for love

Fleshing out the topography of your hand for love starts with the mounts of Venus, that big mound at the base of your thumb, and the lunar mount on the percussive side of your hand. Turn your attention to both of these areas first, because your mount of Venus shows you how you express love, while your lunar mount tells you more about how you receive it. Look, also, at the Saturn, Apollo, and Mercury mounts together under your middle, ring, and pinkie fingers respectively. Saturn had a lot more to do with marriage in palmistry in the past, and still does in cultures where arranged marriage is standard, because it has to do with marital and familial obligations. Apollo, bright god of the sun, shows you all the love that you will find under the sun; it shows marriages as well as mere dating potentials. Finally, Mercury is where your relationship communication and family planning take place.

Start by examining just those five mounts closely and drawing every dot and lined marking that jumps out at you. Look at the morning checks to remember what dots and small markings mean. Note the colors you see associated with each mount and dot.

For example, is your mount of Venus red, pink, or white? The color of your mount of Venus is a barometer of how much passion and love are free to give in your life right now. If you're a single mom of twin newborns, you may be running on empty as far as your sexual and love passion meter goes, but if you're a single woman on the prowl, you may find yourself overloaded with energy. Check the lunar mount for similar information on your readiness to receive a lover.

Sometimes the heart line will extend to the mount of Jupiter, under your pointer finger, and in some cases a current lover may appear as a mark on that line. Look at your mounts of Saturn and Apollo together. On your mount of Saturn, look for a line to Saturn that branches to form a cross on your mount of Apollo. This is an excellent sign for marriage potential in your current relationship situation. If you don't have a cross under Apollo, it doesn't mean that you will never get married. The cross will appear at the right time and when you're with the right person. If you're in a long-term relationship with somebody and no cross is present, you will come to a crossroads, a decision in that relationship. Look lower under Apollo as well, even beyond the mount, because sometimes crosses that represent serious relationship potentials that could possibly end in marriage will appear lower in the palm than the fleshy mount itself.

On your mount of Mercury, look for horizontal lines coming from the percussive edge of your hand. Each of these lines represents an important relationship up to and including marriage. They are often called "lines of marriage," and if more than one is especially deep, I often caution clients to be careful whom they choose to marry so that they don't end up divorced and married more than once. However, in these modern times when long-term and committed relationships don't necessarily always mean marriage, these lines can simply mean important relationships with a significant other.

The road to love is bumpy and long

Now that you've mapped out the love topography of your hand with these five mounts, let's draw some significant roads to love as lines in your palm. The heart line, of course, the head line, and the destiny line (if you have one) will be our focus now. If present, you should also draw your girdle of Venus and via lascivia. Focus on these two to five lines for now, and ignore all others.

Take a look at your heart line, the topmost of the three major horizontal lines in your palm. Draw your heart line carefully. Take note of its depth; where it starts and ends; and any branches, dots, or other marks that have formed along the line.

The depth of the heart line represents your emotional depth. If your heart line is extremely deep, you may be quite passionate and easily moved to tears. If your heart line is shallow, you may feel or express your emotions in a more subtle way.

A person with a straight heart line is more practical and pragmatic about choosing a lover, while a heart line that is wildly curved indicates that you'll follow your heart anywhere it leads, no matter how crazy.

Where does your heart line end right now? Take note of which finger or mount has the tip of your heart line pointing in its general direction. The associations with that finger and mount are clues to the nature of your heart as well as clues to what sort of person might strike your fancy. Dips, rises, and branches in the lines also have to do with each associated finger. Rises and branches indicate more of those traits, while dips may indicate that you shy away from those traits.

Your head line matters too, of course, in matters of the heart. A longer head line may indeed mean that you take longer to get around to settling on the person you want because you are more detail-oriented. A shorter head line helps you see the big picture and may make you fall in love more quickly, but also might give you higher expectations. Note the branches, rises, and falls in the head line as well, and under which finger they occur.

Your destiny line or rising line to Saturn, if you have one, plays a strong role in love for some people. If your parents or family play a big role in how you learned to love and how you want to integrate a new spouse into your family, the destiny line may have branches to the heart line that can hold clues. If your culture practices arranged marriage, or if the financial stability of your partner is mandatory for you to consider him or her, this line may have important dots and branches as warnings and signs for you. Draw this line carefully, noting its depth, branches, and any dots or markings. For some independent people, the absence of a destiny line or a lack of branching or depth associated with the heart line or lunar or Venus mounts may mean that financial and familial obligations just aren't important to them in a lover.

The presence or absence of a girdle of Venus and a via lascivia on your hand will show you where some of your priorities are in relationships. A girdle of Venus shows your need for the finer things in life—beauty and the arts—when connecting deeply with another person. A via lascivia indicates your capacity for a strong libido that can at times be either distracting or helpful in relationships.

By now, you should have a simplified drawing of the palms of both hands that only depicts five mounts and two to five lines. If you are actively seeking change in the love department of your life, it is a good idea to draw these simplified love diagrams in your palmistry journal each month to keep checking for updates on your path. Now that you have a basic idea of the love layout of your destiny, let's examine some more specific questions about romance that lie in the palms of your hands.

Finding a new lover in the palm of your hand

If you're currently single and attempting to find a new love out there in the world, now you can examine just your passive hand. The reason for this is that if you're single and searching, your eventual love match will be waiting in your destiny line in the palm of your passive hand, rather than at your fingertips in your active hand.

Start by taking a look at your heart line and where it ends, rises, and branches. Does the end point down at your thumb? You're a pretty strong-willed person, so you should seek a lover who allows you to have your own way, while supporting you. Searching for a lover through adventurous dating like singles rock climbing or exotic cruises may be the way to go for you.

Does a rise, branch, or end happen underneath your pointer finger? Chances are you shine in leadership roles.

Your match may also be a manager at his or her workplace or somebody in uniform. Conversely, if you are an extremely strong leader, you may have better luck searching for a "type B" person who likes to sit back and follow your lead.

An end, branch, or rise under your middle finger asks you to look for somebody focused on their career or vocation, as well as somebody who takes on a more traditional role. It means that you may have to take on a traditional role in dating yourself. So if you're a man, get ready to bust out the flowers and chocolates to wine and dine a partner in style, and if you're a woman, get in touch with a feminine way of dressing yourself and see if you can find a way to your lover's heart through his stomach.

Though a heart line is unlikely to end at your ring finger, a branch or rise here indicates that creativity and art are what can make you swoon. Somebody who can woo you with the right love song or lyrics or bond with you on the dance floor is more important.

When will my next love come?

By now, I hope I've impressed upon you the idea that things in your palm and life can change. The timing of your next romance is entirely up to you, and common sense says it can be hurried along by actively seeking the right person, being discriminating, and working on your own problems to love yourself first. It can also be delayed as well, so even if everything in your palm is conducive to a blossoming love life, you can still run off and join a convent or monastery and thumb your nose at that potential destiny. That said, your palm does hold clues about the most auspicious timing for events to happen in your life. Find a cross under your ring finger somewhere on the palm of your passive hand, and then determine when in your life is the lucky timing for that cross. We'll cover more about timing systems in palmistry later.

Eenie-meenie-miney-moe:
Choosing between two or more lovers

If you have already found some potential matches and haven't yet looked at their palms for a comparison, you can easily use the characteristics listed above for finding a match to see which one seems like the strongest candidate. Check forward in the chapter on reading your partner's palm for more thorough analysis that includes comparisons.

For now, check where your heart line ends, branches, or rises. If it ends under Jupiter, the potential lover who has the right balance of a little bit of ambition but willingness to let you take the lead may be best for you. If it ends under Saturn, you'll need the lover who has the most stable career of his own. If your heart line branches or rises significantly under Apollo, you'll need the lover who is closer to your own taste in music and the arts. A rise or branch under Mercury means you need the one who communicates most with you; the strong silent type is less attractive in the long run.

A dip in your heart line can warn you of serious in-compatibility issues with one of your lovers. A dip under

Jupiter means that you may not mesh well with the lover who is more authoritarian, while a dip under Saturn can have a similar meaning, and point out that the lover who is too career-driven will not be the one for you. A dip under Apollo means that no matter how much you may love a Peter Pan type or an impractical artist, you won't be able to hold onto that love forever. A dip under Mercury means that one potential lover may be too manipulative or shrewd for you and would best be kicked to the curb.

If you have a girdle of Venus, this means you're going to need the lover who has the tastes and means to spoil you rather than the one with less of a capacity to please. The presence of a via lascivia means that sexual chemistry really does matter and that you should choose the lover who heats your passion the most, rather than choosing another and hoping that over time your chemistry will grow.

Is a bird in the hand worth two in the bush?

Are you with somebody right now and wondering if this is the person who is meant for you, the soulmate you should stick with forever? Are you wondering whether it is time to hit the road and look for a new love? First, be aware that most peoples' palms show more than one potential for a lover. Take a look at those horizontal relationship lines under Mercury. Most people have more than one, and even more can appear over time. Likewise, unless your heart line is extremely short, you have plenty of time to search for a lover. It is very rare to see someone with no choice but to be alone or go with one person.

Still, there are a few things you can check in order to find reassurance to stick around or confirmation that walking out the door is best. Try looking for compatibility as in the above examples based on the end, rises, dips, and branches of your heart line. Look for that cross under Apollo that indicates a relationship crossroads such as marriage. If you've been hanging around for years waiting for a proposal and haven't seen so much as a tiny, faint cross, it may be time to try your luck elsewhere. Check the color of your mount of Venus. If it is blotchy, bright pink, or burning red, you have a lot of love to give and may not have the proper outlet yet.

These few signs may be just the confirmation needed for your feelings. But if you feel this is a big decision, please consider checking ahead in the section on reading your partner's palm for more incompatibility confirmations before you sign the Dear John (or Jane) letter. If the decision about having children is a sticking point in your relationship, make sure you check the section in this chapter on family planning as well.

Will my ex come back to me?

A question on an ex-wife, ex-husband, ex-boyfriend, or ex-girlfriend is one of the most popular topics I receive when asked for a reading of any kind, palmistry included. In the vast majority of these cases, the outcome is that my clients never get back with their ex-lovers, although they may find deeper and better love elsewhere. However, I can understand the need for closure and to not have to wonder whether you should stick around waiting for an old flame when turning confidently to a new future.

When evaluating whether an ex will rekindle a romance, the benefit of tracking your palms over a long period of time is enormous. Your ex is represented by a marking on your palm, and it is easier to confirm which marking on your palm is your ex if you know what your palm looked like before, during, and after your relationship. Otherwise, it is hard to know whether a cross or relationship line belongs to your ex or a new lover yet to come. So even if you're reading this without having started or broken off a relationship yet, please document your palms now and keep track of how they look each month so you can know which marking is which! Your first step in evaluating an ex is to find him or her on your palm. Try the passive hand first; it contains more of your recent past and destiny. Only move to the active palm if you are planning on contacting your ex or attempting to reunite soon.

First, check your Mercury mount under your pinkie finger for those horizontal lines of relationships that come from the percussive edge of the palm. Only the most important relationships will show up, and some may be longer than others, indicating the relationship's length. Some may be deeper than others, indicating the greater seriousness of the relationship. You may be able to deduce that your ex is one of these lines.

If not, the second place you should check is underneath your ring finger. Check all the way down your palm, as an ex-husband or ex-wife may still linger as a cross right on the mount of Apollo, or in the case of a husband, trail away from Saturn or Apollo as a line through a cross to the lunar mount. Ex-lovers may also be a cross lower on the palm, but still underneath that ring finger.

Still haven't found your ex? It may be that he or she has already faded from your destiny and is gone for good, but there's still the heart line to check. Your ex may appear as a dot or a marking along your heart line. If you're still on good terms with your ex or seem to be making headway into a second romance, look for positive signs such as a cross, circle, oval, square, triangle, or pink dot. If there's still a lot of hurt between you two that needs healing, your ex may be a blue or white dot, trident, grid, or grille.

If you can't find your ex on your palm at all, I'm sorry, but it looks like he or she was an important lesson in your life you have already passed, even if it doesn't feel like you've moved all the way past it. The best thing to do in such circumstances is to try to distract yourself with other pursuits and create boundaries, closure, and distance between the two of you. Your palm has confirmed there is no chance right now of a reunion, so you can rest assured and watch for the signs of a new cross popping up under Apollo to bring you love.

If you have located a mark you are certain is your ex, you can now look for signs of a reunion and start checking that mark daily to see if it is getting deeper and darker—a positive sign for reunion—or fading and becoming more shallow—a negative sign for getting back together. Deep, positive markings near the mark that represents your ex, such as a pink dot, cross, circle, oval, or square, indicate you shouldn't give up yet. He or she may still have something to teach you about love. Negative markings such as a black dot or star indicate that reunion is very unlikely. With signs like a grid, grille, trident, or even a triangle, it shows you have a lot more effort to put into things if you want a relationship with your ex to work. Consider carefully whether the person is worth the time and trouble, as well as whether he or she is willing to put in equal effort.

Check, also, for branches from lines that touch the marking representing your ex. A branch to your heart line is expected. Does the branch look deep and connect to an equally deep and straight heart line? If so, the path to reunion may be just as simple. If the branch or head line is shallow, chained, gapped, or wandering, things between you and your ex are very complicated, and you will have a harder time building the necessary stability and trust for a lasting relationship. A branch to your line of Mercury indicates that renewed and healthy communication will be needed to rebuild your relationship. A branch from a line of Apollo is a positive sign showing that caring is there, but as we know, love is not always all you need. A branch from your destiny line shows that responsibilities, duties, and expectations are in the way, while a branch from Jupiter indicates a personality clash may be the heart of the matter. If a branch from your life line comes into play, there may be practical issues keeping the two of you apart. Branches are not necessarily bad signs; they can show the problem as well as the solution. The trick is to strengthen your energies in that area and to hope that your ex chooses the same. After all, the choice to become a couple again is not completely yours—it is your ex's as well.

Career

You guessed it, the second most common topic for palm readings after love is career. Whether you're trying to find your true vocation in life, looking for a job that pays the bills, or hoping the closest thing to a career you'll find is to be a lottery winner, this section will examine the money that lies in the palms of your hands. As with the love focus, I'd like you to draw just the money and career features of both palms of your hands next, leaving out all the details that have nothing to do with that topic. After we make a general map of your fortune, I'll go over some specific questions you might have about your financial or career outlook.

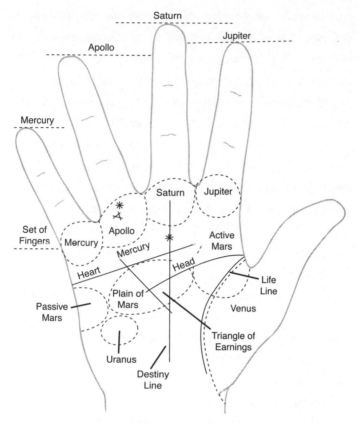

Figure 9: Palmistry for career and money

A map of Treasure Island

Draw the outline of your hand with special care, because
we are going to analyze the shape of your hand, including
its relative width to height and the general shape of your
fingers. Make sure to demarcate the location of each phalange or section of a finger and their relative lengths.

As you draw your thumb, take a look at how wide you can spread your thumb away from your hand, and remember that this is the "angle of generosity" I wrote about previously. Too wide, and money will slip right through your fingers, while if it is too narrow you will find yourself being too stingy to make quality investments and enjoy your earnings properly. Most people fall somewhere in between, meaning that they are practical and careful with borrowing and lending activities. While you're looking at your thumb, press on it to see how quickly the skin bounces back, as this is a measure of your health. If your thumb skin is not very resilient right now, it may recommend that you take a break from working too hard.

Take note of how long your pointer finger is in relation to the rest. A long but evenly-proportioned (meaning with generally equivalent phalanges) Jupiter finger represents an ability to take the lead and take necessary risks with one's own money or the money of others.

Draw the tip and angle of your middle finger carefully. A straight Saturn finger represents somebody with financial discipline. If your Saturn finger leans more toward your pointer finger, you are a self-made person financially. If Saturn bends toward your ring finger, you'll find creative ways to live within your means. A more square tip represents a hard worker, while more rounded or pointed tips mean that your work ethic may falter, especially when it comes to physical labor.

The length of your ring finger, especially if the first phalange is short, represents an inherent ability to assess the value of precious objects. Even if you're not an artist yourself, your Apollo finger can show that you may be able to invest well in collectables, jewelry, or gold. You'll have a knack for knowing when something is pretty, but of little or no value to you.

The length and lean of your pinkie finger, as well as where it sits attached to your palm, relative to the set of the other fingers, has a lot to say about your business sense. If your Mercury finger is long, you have great earning potential. A low-set Mercury finger can represent financial hardship at the beginning of life that can be overcome as an adult. If your Mercury finger leans toward your ring finger, you can be a creative and wealthy business person if you can put some practical action behind your terrific ideas.

Mountains of cash

Next, let's map out the money topography of your palm with the pertinent mounts. Sketch the relative size of the mount of Jupiter under your pointer finger, and draw any lines or markings, dots, or colors you see there. Map the mount of Saturn under your middle finger, taking care to observe any lines, markings, and how large this mount seems to be in the dimensions of width and height in comparison to your other mounts. Draw the mount of Apollo under your ring finger, taking care to make note of any small markings appearing on this mount. Don't forget to map that mount of Mercury under your pinkie finger for size and markings.

Carefully map out your Mars topography, including the valley that is the plain of Mars between your head and heart lines, the top and middle of the three main lines on your palm, and the mounts sandwiching it of passive Mars on the percussive edge of your palm and active Mars on the side of your palm with your thumb. Find and draw the small mount of Uranus as well; it is located just inside of the percussive edge of your hand below the junction between the flat plain of Mars above your head line and the mount of passive Mars along that percussive edge, taking care to note if your head line ends there. Draw any dots or small markings on your Venus mount at the base of your thumb.

If you have a resilient, relatively large mount of Jupiter, you are destined for a leadership role in your career. If you don't find a way to fulfill it, you might make yourself obnoxious in other ways. Positive markings, dots, and colors on Jupiter generally indicate career success, while negative ones indicate barriers to your ability to reach your financial and career goals.

Your mount of Saturn is important for career because it shows your sense of duty. If you have a rising line to Saturn that reaches this mount, you're in good shape as a responsible person. If your mount of Saturn is large and robust, you follow the rules and know how to work within the system. That said, it is not necessarily a bad thing to have a small mount of Saturn—it represents a person who can think outside the box. A strong mount of Saturn can make up for deficiencies in other areas simply because you are consistent and are likely to find steady employment. Note any positive or negative dots, markings, or colors on your mount of Saturn.

If a star and a triad (three markings linked together like a triangle or a trident) both appear on your mount of Apollo, you only need one more sign to suggest a financial windfall may be on its way. Look for a star also appearing on that destiny line, your rising line to Saturn under your middle finger. If all three of these signs appear concurrently, you have winnings, an inheritance, or some other sum of money headed your way. Don't quit your day job yet, though, because the blessing may be small. The size of your mount of Apollo can indicate your talent or skill base, but as we all know from the example of starving artists, raw talent alone isn't enough for financial success. You'll need to take a look at your other mounts to see if you have the business acumen to go with your talents in order to see true profit. Positive markings on Apollo can represent good luck in business or finance, but remember that luck isn't everything, either. If you want the kind of income you can count on every day, look to balance your Apollo energy with that of Saturn. It doesn't hurt to have a strong Apollo when interviewing for a job, but make sure that your sense of drama doesn't sabotage a good thing once you've landed gainful employment.

A full-sized mount of Mercury means you've got enough business sense to make deals and communicate your goals to the people who count. Don't forget that Mercury can have markings that show career clues for you as well, like medical stigmata or the mark of the teacher. A cross on Mercury can represent a business partnership potential. A square on the mount of Mercury is a clue that you need to slow down and balance your career with your life a little more before you run out of vital energy to progress.

Let's examine your Mars topography. Active Mars on the thumb side of your hand represents your ability to control your temper and swallow your pride in order to protect your career and assets. Positive markings, dots, or colors there mean you're doing well. If negative colors, dots, or markings show up, you may need to check yourself. Your plain of Mars shows how you deal with the work the world gives you and whether you perceive it as a blessing or a burden. Your passive Mars shows how well you follow instruction and managerial orders, or how badly you kowtow under pressure, as the case may be. If your head line ends on that tiny mount of Uranus, your inventiveness and creative communication may have a huge potential for making money if they can be practically applied.

The Venus mount shows your deepest material needs and desires. If your values are truly aligned with your spending, you'll see positive dots and markings here. If you're not doing so well, and your money is all being spent on things that don't truly matter or aren't your passions, you'll find more negative markings, dots, and coloration.

Road to riches

Next, let's examine what lines are most important for your career path. Draw your heart line, or topmost, and your head line, or middle, of the three major horizontal lines on your palm, and your life line, which is that third sweeping major line. If you have them, make sure you draw your rising line to Saturn below your middle finger and your rising line to Mercury under your pinkie finger. Take care to note any dots, stars, triangles, tridents, or other markings.

If your heart line has a branch, rise, or end under Saturn, you will have your heart in the right place when it comes to money. That means that you have a natural desire to earn and hold onto money or property, and you need to have a romantic partner who values financial security as well.

Anyone with a disability knows that health has a lot to do with the ability to effectively and consistently earn a living. The depth of your life line shows your healthy energy reserves that you have to put behind your efforts to work hard. Deep life lines can make up for other shortcomings in your work ethic, but shallow life lines mean you'll have to make some accommodations for yourself in order to keep a proper work-life balance.

Check along your destiny line under your middle finger for any stars, and refer to the above section if you find one to look for the other signs that may indicate a financial windfall. A shallow, chained, or broken destiny line is not great news, however, as it can symbolize financial hardship. Take caution if you see signs of your destiny line not looking so strong, and avoid big monetary risks. Branches along your destiny line are all choices that you may have coming up that have to do with your finances or your career. It is good to have choices, so move forward with caution but know that you have options ahead of you and you aren't stuck in an inescapable bind.

Your head line indicates how you think about money. Note any branches that may touch the destiny line. A rise or ending under Saturn can indicate real estate ownership potential. Branches and deepening in this area—especially a head line that ends under Saturn—means that you have a solid head on your shoulders when it comes to money. If your head line shies away from your destiny line, or if you see gaps, shallowness, or chaining, you may need to consult somebody who has a better head for money on occasion.

A brief review of the "triangle of earnings": It is made up of your head line, your destiny line (or rising line to Saturn) and your rising line to Mercury. The larger the triangle, the larger the earning potential. A gap or opening in the triangle can represent a tendency for money to slip out of your grasp.

Which career path is best for me?

The shape of your hand is often a good indicator of the collection of skills and abilities that make you a good worker. Hand shapes have different labels and are often especially suited to certain vocations or tasks. Rarely are hands a textbook example of a single shape, so you may find that you excel in a variety of careers related to aspects of your hands that fit several different categories of hand shapes. In the following paragraphs, I will describe a system of hand shapes developed in the last century, but be aware that there are other hand shape systems as well, one of which will be described later on in the section on personality characteristics (p. 142).

If your hands are large and have blunt features, short fingers, and wide nails, you may have an elementary hand. Elementary hands are sometimes rough, with faint and short lines. People with elementary hands are well-suited for careers as gardeners, jewelers, plumbers, metal workers, truckers, or working with animals.

If your hands are shaped like squares or long rectangles with square fingers, smooth skin, and deep lines, you may have a practical hand. People with practical hands would do well as architects, entrepreneurs, nurses, teachers, and managers.

If your hands are generally square or wide rectangles, with big joints and flat fingertips, you may have a spatulate hand shape. Spatulate hands are thick with deep lines. Those with spatulate hands could excel as engineers, computer programmers, carpenters, artists, musicians, mechanics, and project managers.

If your hands are generally triangular (wider at the base than at the fingers) with long fingers that may have cone tips, you may have conic hands. Conic hands are graceful and smooth in appearance and may have many meandering lines. People with conic hands are generally good artists, designers, decorators, writers, lawyers, and problem-solvers.

If your hands are generally long oval shapes with fingers that are long with pronounced joints and tips, you may have a philosophical hand. Philosophical hands have firm palms with many deep lines. People with philosophical hands do well as inventors, analysts, therapists, critics, philosophers, reviewers, writers, and scientists.

If your hands are long and slender ovals with long and thin fingers, you may have the psychic hand type. Psychic hands are smooth and sometimes pale with many lines. Those with psychic hands are given to careers as psychics, spiritual leaders, poets, artists, writers, and philosophers.

Mixed hands are a true mishmash of two or more hand types that are not a subtle blend at all. It may appear as if some fingers on the same hand belong to two different people, as if they have been grafted on or cobbled together. People with mixed hands can do well at any career in life, but may find themselves switching from one to another frequently.

Your hand shape isn't the only indicator of your job potential. Take a closer look at your drawing. Look at each of the mounts, paying special attention to areas in which you shine that are marked with crosses, triangles, and even sometimes stars, although stars can represent a lot of energy in that area which can end in triumph or trouble.

Positive marks on your Jupiter mount, under your pointer finger, show that you would do well if self-employed, a boss or CEO, or working fairly independently. On the Saturn mount under your middle finger are marks that point out more of a team player, someone who can survive and thrive in large corporations or government work. Good markings on your mount of Apollo under your ring finger mean you're an artist at heart, while positive markings on your Mercury mount under your pinkie finger indicate an intellectual occupation like a teacher, writer, medical professional, or business person. Check also for good signs on your lunar mount on the percussive edge of your palm, which can indicate an emotional and interpersonal career like a therapist, counselor, spiritual advisor, or artist.

Will I get a raise or a promotion?

In addition to working on enlarging your triangle of earnings, as discussed in the previous chapter, you can look at branches on your destiny line (if you have one) to see career opportunities. The lower on your palm the branches, the more distant these career opportunities may be from you in time. So if you're trying to decide whether to leave your current job or stick around and wait for it to get better, you can analyze branches in the destiny line to make your choice.

For example, if you have many deep branches splitting from your destiny line, it means that you are in a position of power right now since you have many opportunities available to you. A person with many branches on the destiny line can afford to make ultimatums and shop around for a better job openly while discussing a pay raise with the boss. If, however, you have no branching, or your only branch is very low on the palm and reaching for the life line, it may indicate that you would have to jump through more hoops. Such a branch reaching toward the life line might suggest that a move to a new city or even a career change would be necessary in order to make change, so you should be more cautious about leaving your current position of employment.

Will I win the lottery?

Sorry, the winning lotto numbers are not written on your hand; don't let any palm reader tell you differently and offer a pricey palm reading to find out more. If that were the case, I would be too busy rolling in my own piles of money to write this book. However, there are three signs mentioned previously that, when seen together, portend a financial windfall—small *or* large. These are a star and a triad (triangle or trident) on your mount of Apollo under your ring finger as well a star on your destiny line rising up to your middle finger. If you have all three of these, it is a great idea to start buying lottery tickets on a regular basis. Otherwise, don't worry; I don't have these signs either and neither do most people. The rest of us will have to keep earning a living the hard way.

Your family

Everyone in your life shows up on your palm at some point. Some people make deep lines on your hand that last a lifetime, even after they've left this earth. Others are transient and may fade from your hands as they fade from your memory. By now, you may be a pro at noticing colors, dots, and small markings happening that mean big things. Now, I'd like you to draw a map of your family members on your hand so that the proximity of those markings may take on new meaning as changes happen in your relationship. Look on your passive hand for how these people affect your life and your personality overall, and check your active hand if you have a current pressing issue with a family member. Draw both hands for now to make a map, as usual. Some family members may show up on one hand but not the other.

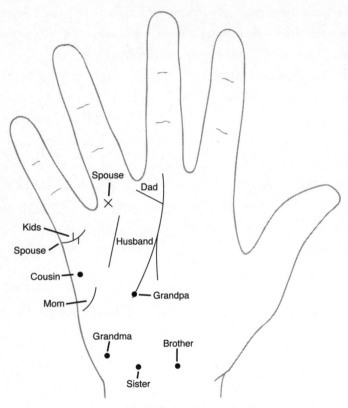

Figure 10: Palmistry for your family

Mom: A red or pink line on the lunar mount on the percussive side of your hand.

Dad: A line or branch from your destiny line on your mount of Saturn under your ring finger.

Kids: On your Mercury mount, underneath your pinkie finger, rising or descending perpendicular to relationship lines that lie horizontally from the percussive edge of your palm.

Sister: Markings found on the mount of Pluto at the base of your palm on the inside of the lunar mount (found on the lower percussive edge of your palm). Your sisters, or spiritual sisters, can be shown as any lines or dots.

Brother: Markings found on the mount of Pluto at the base of your palm on the inside of your mount of Venus (found at the base of your thumb).

Grandma: Markings found within the lunar mount at the lower percussive edge of your palm.

Grandpa: Markings found at the lower end of your destiny line (rising line to your middle finger), or can also appear as a branch on your mount of Saturn from that same line.

Cousin: Markings found above your lunar mount, at the lower percussive edge of your palm.

Wife: Either a cross on your mount of Apollo under your ring finger or a horizontal line under your pinkie finger coming from the percussive edge of your hand, or both.

Husband: Same as the signs for a wife above, or can also be
a rising line from your lunar mount (on the lower percussive edge of your hand) to either your middle finger
or ring finger.

Lover: A serious lover whom you simply may not have in-
ducted into your family in any other way can be shown
as an Apollo cross in your hand low under your ring
finger. He or she may also be found as a mark along the
heart line, especially one on the mount of Jupiter under
your pointer finger.

Can I talk to my deceased loved one through palmistry?
Your beloved ancestors are still holding your hand every
step of your way in life, even if they have died. Watch your
active hand for messages from a deceased loved one appearing near the marking associated with the family member
that you have found listed above. For example, a deceased
father giving his blessing for a wedding might appear as a
pink dot appearing on a branching line from his daughter's
destiny line on her wedding day. If you have a special person on the other side who is close to you, consider adding
to your morning palmistry checks a moment to ask out
loud for his or her guidance, and then look at the area of
your dominant hand palm that he or she can use to send
you messages from beyond.

Will I ever have a better relationship
with my estranged family member?

Take a look at your destiny line rising up toward your middle finger. Is it frayed or broken? It could be that you have some strained family relationships, and if you apologize or make amends, you'll see that rising line to Saturn change to develop a protective square, become more solid, and perhaps even lengthen. Likewise, look at the family chain wrapped around the base of your thumb. If this chain is broken or thinned, it indicates that the degree of physical or emotional separation from your family may be the culprit, and working on becoming closer can complete the chain over time.

Now that you know the areas and markings of your palms that are associated with each family member, you can also track your relationships with them as they happen on the active hand, or your destiny as it is forming with them on your passive hand. So if you are having trouble with a specific family member, you can often find the root of the trouble as well as potential outcomes written on your passive hand. Since relationships with family members can take a lifetime to manage, pay extra special attention to family member markings that occur along lines in the hand, or that have branches to lines on the hand. Here are some examples:

Father or mother: First, are there any badly colored dots around that family member's mark? A black, yellow, or blue dot can mean serious sickness, substance abuse, or mental illness may be a problem with your relationship. A white dot may mean the problem has more to do with ineffective or inconsistent communication. A grid or grille can represent a more physical or practical barrier came between you, such as finances or a situational problem that can be overcome. If a trident is there, you may be even closer to one of you making the right choices to renew a relationship. The solution may be simply to set healthy boundaries, allowing the person with the choice to take the chance and make it on his or her own terms. Stars can be tricky, since they represent a personality clash that may take a lifetime of management.

For your mother, check to see if that pink line that represents her on the lunar mount has any branching lines from the life line pointing toward it. The condition of your life line may represent your journey getting to know your mom, and as you move down lower on your palm you can see your progress. Is the condition of the line getting better or worse? Likewise, for your father, the destiny line rising up toward your middle finger will show the progress of your relationship. Looking from the top of your hand to the bottom again, you can read the condition of the line and see if it looks like it is improving. Remember, both these lines can change over time as you work on your relationships.

Kids: From their position on the Mercury mount under your pinkie finger, in addition to the dots and markings that you should check as described above for moms and dads, your children may be touched by branches from the heart line, head line, or rising line to Mercury. If your heart line is in bad shape, chaining and shallow or gapped, it may mean that your relationship with your kids can be improved by improving on your relationship with others. For example, perhaps leaving a bad partnership with a spouse or mending bad feelings between you and an ex who is also a parent to your kids may be needed. If your head line is the one in trouble, you may have some habits of thinking about your kids that lead to trouble. The way you were raised or the emotional strain of your life may have overcomplicated things so that you have ideological differences. Counseling and therapy can help mend head line issues with your children. If your Mercury line is in trouble, communication is the key, and you may need outside help from a therapist or counselor.

Siblings: Again, check for the markings surrounding your brothers and sisters that are mentioned in the analysis of your relationship with Mom and Dad. From their vantage point at the base of the palm, your sibling relationships can easily be influenced by branches from your life line, destiny line, or rising line to Mercury. As with children, work on communication if it is the

Mercury line poking in. If the destiny line is in poor condition and touches a brother or sister, it may be that your relationship with your parents strains your relationship with your brothers and sisters. If your life line has branches that touch a sibling, your own energy level and ability to cope with their problems may not be sufficient at this time, or it could be barriers of time and space that come between you.

How many kids will I have?

If you read the section on love, you have probably already taken note of the horizontal lines coming from the percussive edge of your hand on the mount of Mercury. These are relationship lines, and they represent important relationships like marriages and long-term partnerships. Now, take a look to see if any smaller lines sprout up or down perpendicular to those relationship lines. Such lines represent children, but before you run out and buy a pregnancy test, know that lines of children get complicated.

Are the child lines not quite touching the relationship lines from which they seem to sprout? There may be several reasons for this disconnect. It may be that the relationship from which those children spring does not last. Just because you divorce a partner doesn't mean you divorce your children, after all. It may also mean that those kids are not necessarily biologically a result of that relationship, even if they really do become a part of your life because of it. Such children may be adopted, or could be stepchildren from a previous marriage. In the case of people who are teachers, or even just take on a teaching role with children in their lives, detached child lines can appear speckled all over the mount of Mercury. These can be nieces, nephews, neighborhood kids, or pupils.

Gender is tricky, too. There are several schools of thought on how to interpret this; one is that if the lines slant toward Apollo, the child is a girl, while lines slanting away from Apollo are boys. Another interpretation is that lines pointing up from the relationship lines are boys or have masculine, dominant personality traits. Lines pointing down are girls or have passive, traditionally feminine personality traits.

Planning a family? If you're still undecided about having kids, if you're without a parenting partner, if you are young, or if having a family is still far off in the future, check in with your passive hand to keep track of your destiny. Lines of children on your passive hand represent all the children that you're destined to have as the course of your life is headed now. Even if you are infertile, remember that adopted kids and other children of your heart can be present as child lines.

A brief warning about a rascette around the wrist rising into the palm: on a woman, this sign used to mean an inability to have biological children, or a potential for death during childbirth. Modern obstetrical care has largely decreased the incredible mortality rate that used to be associated with childbirth in olden times. However, it is still an indication that the best medical care should be sought throughout family planning.

If you're trying to conceive, possibly pregnant, or pregnant and wanting to find out the gender of your current baby, or whether you're having twins, look on your active hand for the fastest changing and latest updates on the news regarding your family planning.

Health

Of course, a palm reading is no substitute for going to the doctor. However, palmistry systems have described changing health situations for as long as they have been in existence. There are a few good signs for a health reading of the hand. One is a healthy pink color, another is a deep life line with positive signs along it. Your rising line to Mercury, called a hepatica, is also considered your health line, but ironically it is a good sign for health if you don't have one at all, because it means health doesn't have to be your focus and may come naturally or be rolled into your healthy life line. However, if you do have one, it is good to be at the other extreme and have a long health line, indicating longevity brought about from a focus on healthy living. Marks along the health line can indicate health issues or healing influences, and chaining may indicate digestive problems that can be aided by proper nutrition. A tassel or many fraying forks at the end of the hepatica or life line indicate the natural decay of health associated with old age.

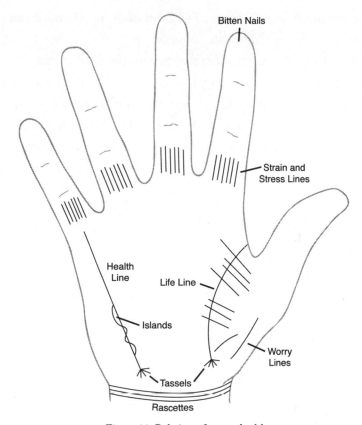

Figure 11: Palmistry for your health

Stress is a big influence on health that can be found easily in the palm. Worry lines radiating out from the base of the thumb that cross the life line are indications that anxiety is beginning to have physical effects. More strain and stress lines may be found on the base phalange of each finger, indicating stresses in the physical realm. If those fingers are topped off with bitten fingernails, you've got a case where somebody really has to manage mental issues before their health begins to suffer.

It was once believed by the Romany people that each rascette, or bracelet at the base of the palm on the wrist, indicated a potential for twenty-five more years of longevity. As with any other death timing prediction on the palm, things can change, and it has been pointed out by some that the rascette method is suspect because almost everybody has numerous rascettes.

When will things happen in my life?

There are several timing systems that assess the life line's relationship to other features on the hand to estimate time. Remember, as with anything else in palmistry, your life line can change and the timing of life events will also change as a result. If you determine the timing of an event in your life that is important to you, reassess it monthly to see if it is still on track or getting waylaid by your choices. I suggest using a piece of string for quick measurement.

For example, if you see a cross under Apollo indicating a relationship on either your heart line or your life line, measure that distance with a string starting from the beginning of that line and then cutting the string right where the cross exists. Label the string with a piece of tape indicating that it is the cross under Apollo. Each month you can pull out that string and easily lay it across the line to make sure that your line or cross haven't moved. If either has, it will be easy to see whether you're going to be getting to that relationship more quickly if you have an excess of string now, or if you're going to have to wait longer if your string no longer quite reaches.

Life line timing

Your tenth year of life can be found by imagining a line running down the middle of your pointer finger into your life line, according to French palmist Henri Mangin. Your twenty-first year of life is depicted on your palm by an imaginary line you can draw straight down from the junction between your pointer finger and your middle finger.

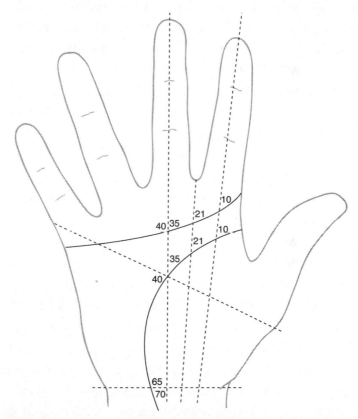

Figure 12: Life line timing

Some believe that age thirty-five is a diagonal imaginary line drawn straight from the base of your pinkie finger on the percussive edge of your hand. Others believe this age is found by an imaginary line from the very middle of the middle finger, although Mangin believed the Saturn line's mark to be age forty. Which one is right for you? You'll be able to determine the best timing system for you by comparing potential timing with events that have already happened, which I'll explain soon. Depending on the shape of your lines, some imaginary lines may or may not cross your life line at all, which eliminates them for timing purposes.

Your potential sixty-fifth year of life may be an imaginary horizontal line across the bottom of your palm through the base of your thumb. Remember, most everyone has this part of the hand, even if they are not going to ever reach this age of life. Some believe that age seventy is shown by where the life line starts to go backward around the base of the thumb.

Now that you've drawn those imaginary lines, you can infer where other years are along your heart line and life line. By noting other markings that you recognize as significant events in your life, you can make further notes as reference points. For example, if you've experienced a significant difficult life event such as a divorce, you can look for a star on the heart line and write the year of your divorce in your notes on that point. Similarly, if you experienced a serious injury or illness, you can look for a mark like a black dot on your life line and note the year there. Fill in as many year numbers as you can, and you'll create little rulers on your lines that can tell you the approximate years that events in your life are likely to happen. Now you can predict things as well. For example, when you see any cross appear under Apollo, you can now have proper reference points to gauge the timing of an upcoming relationship.

Some palmists use math to determine timing along the life line. For example, if you measure the length between the age of thirty-five on the life line and the age of seventy and then divide that length by two, you'll find the spot at which you are halfway through your fifty-second year of life. You can keep dividing this line to narrow down to specific year markings along the line. You can also start dividing by measuring from the beginning of the life line to age seventy, and then dividing that in half and marking the resulting point as age thirty-five.

Desbarrolles timing system

If the above life line reference timing just isn't working for you, particularly if your life line doesn't hit any of those markers due to a short length or gaps, you may wish to try another method with a geometrical compass to draw a circle on your palm. The Desbarrolles method works best if your life line doesn't happen to hug close to your thumb or reach way out across your palm.

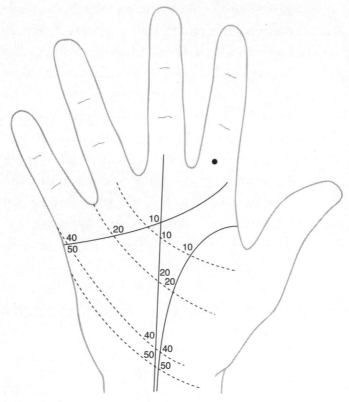

Figure 13: Desbarrolles timing system

The center point of the circle should be at the middle of the base of your pointer finger, while the edge of the circle begins at the middle of the base of your ring finger. Where the circle's imaginary line intersects your life line should be the tenth year of your life.

The twentieth year of your life in the Desbarrolles method is shown when you draw a circle starting the edge from the junction between your ring and pinkie fingers.

The fortieth year of your life is drawn from the far edge of your pinkie finger. Your fiftieth year is marked starting where your heart line meets the edge of your palm.

Cheiro's timing system

Do you have tricky lines that seem to shy away from all the imaginary lines drawn from various other hand features? Palmist Cheiro avoided referencing any other points on the palm by simply measuring the lines themselves, which you can do with a string, and then dividing the lengths into ten equal parts, each representing a period of seven years.

Julius Spier's timing system

Are there marks on your life line that seem to indicate that you're looking at the timing backward? In that case, try dating events from the wrist up. Divide the life line in two, and that mark represents the twentieth year of your life. You can find all the other years using further division.

Special timing systems
for the destiny and heart lines

You might find that if you draw invisible lines or divide up the life line, the timing you find seems to match with signs that indicate important events in your life, but the rising line to Saturn and the heart line don't quite seem to match up. Here are a couple of specialized timing systems just for them. Where the destiny line crosses the head line is age thirty-five, and where it passes the heart line is forty-five. You can now make further inferences from these points.

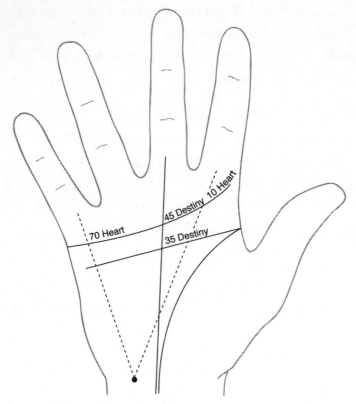

Figure 14: Special timing systems for the destiny and heart lines

For your heart line, try the Romany timing method of drawing invisible lines from the middle of the bases of your Jupiter finger and your Mercury finger to the midpoint of your wrist. Where the Jupiter imaginary line crosses the heart line is age ten, and where the Mercury imaginary line crosses is age seventy. You can experiment with inferring other ages from the rest of the line.

Working on your personality

You are in charge of your own destiny. I feel an exciting sense of responsibility and power when I make changes after seeing a potential fate written in the palms of my hands, and then see the corresponding changes in my life and in my subsequent palmistry readings. But we all know that some people have an easier time than others finding love, landing the perfect job, or getting along with friends and family. Personality characteristics are difficult (if not impossible) to change. Some personality characteristics such as our general activity level, reaction to new external things, and general demeanor may be the same as they were when we were tiny babies, or even before birth.

The fact that some things are fixed in life does not mean you have to sit there and do nothing in life. I like to think of destiny and personality characteristics as a framework within which there is some flexibility. As a metaphor, think of fate as a system of one-way roads. You can still turn your car right or left, bringing you to an entirely different destination, but there are set points to which you can travel. It does no good to crash into a barrier on the side of the road or drive yourself off a bridge, but you can slow your car down and make a turn at a crossroads, or step on the gas and stay on the freeway. The point of using palmistry to find those more fixed or slowly changing characteristics, like personality, is to know what the roads look like so you can plan which route you would prefer to take, and think about how hard the construction project might be to change those roads.

Palmistry to observe, define, and refine character traits

Knowing yourself is an important aspect of being empowered. When you know your abilities and limitations, you can stop spending all of your efforts on fruitless endeavors and start carefully spreading out more of your time on activities that come easily to you and self-improvements that are possible but require more work. Exploring your personality might feel a little embarrassing or even saddening at times, but don't get discouraged. I'd like to start by showing you a lot of positive personality traits and innate characteristics that you might see in the palm of your hand, so don't skip this part even if you know you have a lot of self-improvements to make. Knowing your worth and value is your foundation for all betterment, so don't shy away from taking pride in the following positive signs. Thank yourself, your upbringing, your support system, and the gods for what you have. File away all of these helpful tools in your arsenal to do battle with your dark side later on.

Playing to your strengths

Draw your passive hand carefully so that you can take note of your hand shape. Hand shapes were introduced in the last chapter, in the section on finding your ideal career, and they hold a lot of clues about your more stable personality type.

Elementary: A palm that is large and rough with wide and short fingers that have square tips. Lines are few, and generally short and straight. You are a hard-working person with plenty of energy to put behind your efforts. You excel at things that are hands-on, physical, and having to do with nature.

Practical: A palm that is a smooth square or a long rectangle with short fingers that have square tips. Lines are deep. You are honest, decisive, practical, and consistent, but patient as you persevere. You excel at things that are active, down-to-earth, and precise. This hand is called the "metal hand" in some elemental hand shape systems in palmistry.

Spatulate: A thick square or widely rectangular palm with long fingers that have flattened tips. The lines are deep. You are competent, social, likable, and have a confident, can-do attitude. You excel at mechanical and visually spatial tasks.

Conic: A smooth, triangular palm with long fingers that have pointed tips. Lines are wandering and numerous. You are imaginative, original, passionate, and full of creativity.

Philosophical: A long, oval palm with long fingers and many deep lines. You are extroverted, diplomatic, analytical, and motivated to be physically active. You excel at things that are intellectual, scholarly, and cultural. This hand is called the "wood hand" in some elemental systems of palmistry.

Psychic: A long, slender palm that is full of lines with long, thin fingers. You are mystical, imaginative, idealistic, intuitive, and contemplative. Your strengths are in all things spiritual.

Mixed: A truly mixed hand seems like it is cobbled together from several different pieces of other hands. Most hands are not truly mixed, but just a single hand type that may be blended on the spectrum toward another. You seem to be made up of many different traits and are adaptable, versatile, mobile, and friendly. You excel at things that require flexibility and being social.

Still don't think your hand fits into any of those categories, or are you hungry for another way of understanding your personality? There is another, more modern system of hand classification that divides hands into only four categories, instead of the classic seven listed above. Note that these aren't added hands, so it was intended that hands from all seven classic categories should fall into only these four. You can switch to the four modern hand classifications if you find them more simple or sensible. Some people add two other elements, wood and metal, which are the same as the philosophical and practical hands respectively in the classical palmistry system.

Earth: A square palm with short fingers, few but deep lines. Those with earth hands are reliable, careful, and practical. They enjoy working with their hands and with the earth. Positive blessings of people with earth hands include a long, healthy life.

Air: A square palm with long fingers. People with air hands are detail-oriented, thoughtful, intuitive, logical, expressive, sociable, and inquisitive. People with air hands enjoy challenges, travel, communicating, freedom, and anything quirky and unique.

Fire: A long rectangular or oval palm with short fingers. People with fire hands are imaginative, versatile, enthusiastic, energetic, social, and busy. Fire-handed folks enjoy looking at the big picture, varying tasks, and having their social and work plates full.

Water: A long rectangular or oval palm with long fingers. Those with water hands are artistic, imaginative, idealistic, versatile, and loving. Water-handed people love art, living things, and being creative.

Strong fingers

Length equals strength in palmistry when it comes to the fingers, but if you've got tiny hands and short fingers like I do, that doesn't mean that you don't have any positive qualities. It is the relative lengths that are important. For example, start by looking at the phalanges or segments of each of your fingers. Naturally, hands are proportioned so that the base phalange is a little bigger than the middle phalange, which is a little bigger than the fingertip phalange. However, many hands vary greatly.

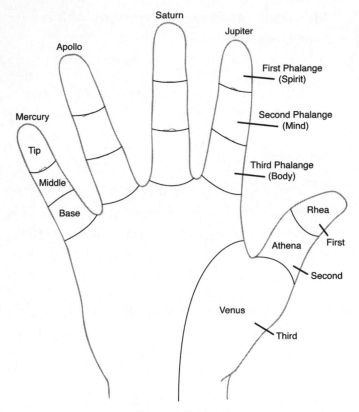

Figure 15: Phalanges

Is the fingertip segment longer than the middle or base ones? If so, that means you are both expressive and intuitive. If the middle one seems longer than the base phalange, it means you are rational and patient. If your base phalange is very long in comparison to the others, you have strong physical energy and may be good at managing material and financial things.

A long or fat thumb represents somebody with a strong force of will. If your thumb is bigger than most, or if it reaches almost to the knuckle of your pointer finger when flattened against the hand, you have the willpower to tackle any task. The tip phalange of the thumb is associated with the goddess Rhea and willpower, while the middle phalange is Athena—logic. The mount of Venus acts as the third phalange for the thumb, therefore a fat mount of Venus indicates that you have a lot of love to give.

Your Jupiter finger is considered to be long if it reaches past the bottom of Saturn's nail, showing that you are a fine leader. Ideally, it won't be too long, allowing you to be okay with following the directions of others if they're good ideas. If your pointer finger leans inward toward Saturn, you are an incredibly resourceful person who works well within a system or organization. If that Jupiter finger leans away from your hand, you have more of a unique style that can allow you to set new trends and think outside the box.

The length of your Saturn finger represents how serious you are, and how disciplined when it comes to things like work and finances. It is okay if another finger approaches the same length as your middle finger. After all, you need to have some sense of fun and play. But a long Saturn finger means you'll certainly have the drive to succeed in your career, even if it is a difficult one. If your Saturn finger leans toward Apollo, you'll do well helping people in your job or financially through charity. If your middle finger leans toward your Jupiter finger, you will excel at independent work or even at being a boss or entrepreneur.

An incredibly long Apollo or ring finger is not necessarily a good thing. Hopefully yours doesn't stick out too far, but is long enough to give you a good taste for the arts and appreciation for beauty. If your ring finger leans toward Saturn, you tend to go with the flow and have many who share your interests, while a lean toward Mercury indicates a unique artistic flair.

People with long Mercury fingers are clever, fast talkers, and excellent writers. They are likely to have excellent business sense and are motivated by money. If your Mercury finger happens to be set high on the palm, which is quite rare, that means exceptional skill in communication and commerce. If that Mercury finger is straight but leans inward toward the ring finger, you are excellent at reading people, especially in matters of business and finances.

Strong lines

As was explained in the section on love (p. 95), the area where your heart line ends or where you find little peaks can show you your attitudes about love and lovers. A curved heart line is a good sign, as the peaks show your values depending on which finger lies above the peak. Even dips are a good sign, because they show a sense of practicality in that there are some people you will avoid because you know they are no good for your heart.

While the ending point of a head line can change, the origin of the head line is an important and rather inflexible palm characteristic. Many peoples' head line starts joined with their life line, which makes sense because at the beginning of your life, both the nature of your life's energies and your way of thinking are often shaped by your family. Some head lines begin just below the life line and cross it, indicating a close connection to family that may even have begun in a past life, and a person who tends to be an "old soul" or mature beyond his or her years. As with the heart line, a curve in the head line is a good thing. The steeper the downward curve, the greater the indication of an active imagination. A straight head line isn't as difficult a challenge as a straight heart line, however, because it indicates somebody with purpose and consistency. The straight heart line is covered below in the "weak lines" section.

Where does your life line originate? They all begin between the thumb and pointer finger, but if they start up high on the Jupiter mount, this emphasizes the way you blaze an independent and new path in life from your own dynamic sense of leadership. A lower origin, from active Mars, shows a sense of competitiveness and strong, almost restless energy in your zest for life. Ideally, your life line will have a graceful, smooth curve, indicating you glide through the challenges and changes life throws at you with integrity and competence. It doesn't matter if your life line hugs close to your thumb or departs from it, though it can indicate whether you like to stick close to home, or adventure far and wide over the course of your life, respectively.

The rest of the rising lines in your hand, if you even have them, are more changeable, but it is nice to be off to a good start with your destiny line, rising line to Apollo, rising line to Jupiter, and rising line to Mercury. If your destiny line rising up to your middle finger doesn't go through your head and heart lines, or breaks as it does, it can actually be a good thing—it means you aren't too serious about your duties and can have some fun. Plenty of branches from the destiny line indicate how resourceful you are when it comes to career and family. The existence of a long hepatica or rising line to Mercury is a good thing: it aids your communications and puts your focus on a healthy lifestyle that can lead to longevity. Believe it or not, the absence of a hepatica is a good thing, too, since it may mean health comes naturally to you without thinking about it. An Apollo line or sun line helps with successful artistic discernment and talents and a Jupiter line gives you power as an advisor, leader, and critic.

Another small blessing in the form of a line is the sympathy line, appearing as a straight horizontal line on the mount of Jupiter directly below the pointer finger. This indicates that you are an understanding person with a very tolerant outlook on life that can help you get along with people and have less stress than others. An even better sign of carefree friendship is the sign of the butterfly, a horizontal hourglass found in the middle of the palm with one end along the life line.

Leaving your mark
of greatness with fingerprints

To find some unchanging lines in your hand, we'll have to go smaller, so get out your magnifying glass. Dermato-glyphics is the study of your fingerprint patterns (also called whorls) on your skin, which stay relatively unchanged throughout the course of your life. I suggest getting an ink pad and recording your handprints in your palmistry journal. It may be messy and difficult to do without smudging, but dematoglyphics are luckily one aspect that you don't have to watch for change. Notice I said *handprints*, not just fingerprints. That's because you also have those tiny whorls everywhere on your palm's surface. The presence of whorls on your mounts is important and unchanging even if your mounts change in size around them.

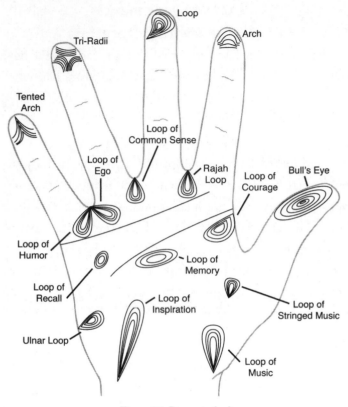

Figure 16: Dermatoglyphs

Everyone has a whorl on each fingertip, but in general, the more whorls you have on the rest of your palm, the better. Check at the base in between each finger, right where they are joined. Do you have any of those whorls at all on your active Mars? This gives you courage during any sort of confrontation, challenge, or battle—literal or figurative. A whorl at the junction between your pointer finger and middle finger is called the mark of royalty, and shows strong family ties and an immense sense of responsibility toward kin and loved ones. A whorl at the junction between your middle and ring fingers is called the mark of nobility, showing that you are a champion for the less fortunate and animals. Finally, a whorl at the juncture between your ring and pinkie fingers is the mark of humor, showing a sharp sense of wit.

A whorl found between your mounts of Venus and the moon, lower in the palm, indicates a strong sibling bond, while a whorl found on the mount of Uranus (between your lunar mount and the junction between active Mars and the plain of Mars) can show a strong inventive energy that drives you to create and build things. Just make sure you channel that energy to appropriate hobby and career potentials instead of leading yourself to distraction. Let's take a look at the types of whorls you might see and the personality strengths they reveal.

Arch: An upward wave is an arch, and shows somebody stable and reliable, with a good work ethic. An especially high arch is called a tented arch; it adds enthusiasm and impulse to the person's drive to create or succeed.

Bull's-eye: A round whorl of concentric circles indicates independence, an analytical nature, ambition, motivation, and persistence.

Loop: A more elongated or misshapen whorl is considered a loop, and is the sign of someone adaptable and flexible to many situations. Loops found in specific locations on the palm may bless the person with specific personality strengths, which will be described in a bit.

Tri-radii: Also known as apexes, this is where three arch waves come together at their apexes to form a sort of triangle shape. The tri-radii shows a person with powerful spiritual and psychic energy.

Loops lassoing strong blessings

Loop of common sense: Also called the loop of good intent, found at the junction between your ring finger and middle finger, if you have this loop it shows that you are responsible and industrious.

Loop of courage: Found on active Mars, at the junction between the thumb and pointer finger under the life line, this loop gives its bearer bravery.

Loop of humor: This loop is found at the junction between your ring and pinkie fingers, and drops down into the mount of Mercury, rather than slanting toward Apollo like the loop of ego. Its presence indicates somebody blessed with an unusual sense of humor.

Loop of inspiration: This mark of greatness begins at the base of the palm at the wrist, and lies up on the mount of Neptune on the interior edge of the lunar mount.

People with the rare loop of inspiration are inspired by things that affect them emotionally, and they often create great things from such inspiration.

Loop of memory and loop of recall: Found in the very center of the palm running diagonally or horizontally lengthwise underneath the head line, the loop of memory indicates somebody with an accurate memory for details. The loop of recall, between the head and heart lines and usually under the junction between ring and pinkie fingers, helps people instantly recall large amounts of information.

Loop of music and loop of stringed music: Beginning at the base of the wrist on the edge of the hand below the thumb, on the mount of Venus, the loop of music gives a person musical talent. The loop of stringed music in the center of the mount of Venus gives a person a special appreciation for listening to stringed instruments.

Rajah loop: Traditionally an indication of royal descent in Indian palmistry, this loop found at the junction between your pointer and middle fingers shows charisma and honor.

Ulnar loop: Starting on the percussive edge of the hand and swirling onto the lunar mount, this loop shows a person deeply in touch with his or her subconscious and with a special gift for loving nature.

Self-improvements

Draw your passive palm now to take notes of those personality traits that may not be so positive, so you can know what sort of changes to make in your life based on what's lasting or what's simply not meant to be. Look at the section above or the glossary to refresh yourself on the meanings of these parts of the hand. We'll start again with hand shapes; see if you can identify with and embrace a few character quirks that might cause you to rethink how you apply yourself.

Elementary: This is a person who can be stubborn and plodding. Even though the name of the shape of this hand is elementary, think of the four natural elements rather than of an elementary school teacher. For you, the jobs and people that force you to make quick decisions and changes are not going to work out well. Instead, turn your slow pace into an asset by applying yourself to employment, hobbies, and friendships that appreciate your tendency to stop and smell the roses.

Practical: Blunt and a perfectionist, the person with a practical hand can easily offend others. Think before you speak and write, or run it by a trusted friend before you send a letter or make an important phone call. Your honesty and sense of what is right is best applied to yourself first rather than to others.

Spatulate: Some people might find those with spatulate hands to be a bit shallow. Getting into deep philosophical or intellectual conversations may seem boring to you, and political debates are the opposite of fun. Stay away from jobs and people that seem to overthink simple matters. Pick activities that allow you to occupy your hands while others find the joy in just being around you.

Conic: Impractical, physically lazy, insincere, sensitive, and impulsive. Have you been accused of any of those qualities, especially during your teenage years? The best way to avoid the pitfalls of having conic hands is to work as a part of a team. You'll need coworkers, friends, and family to let you know when you need to change your attitude or step back from an idea, but you'll be able to inspire others to do the sort of work that makes you feel bored or frustrated.

Philosophical: Extravagant and reclusive, those with philosophical hands may come off as snooty or aloof. Seek friendships and relationships with others who enjoy their space, independence, and the finer things in life, else you'll find the more clingy types become resentful of you. When your social life feels too frustrating or nonexistent, go ahead and throw yourself into your work. The distraction of a job well done and the rewards that come from it will bring you satisfaction.

Psychic: Physically weak, impractical, and overwhelmed are how those with psychic hands feel in their darkest moments. Because you are so sensitive and in tune with others, you find yourself trying to help too much and can easily get bogged down and unable to help yourself…much less anyone else. Do apply yourself to helpful jobs and volunteer work, but know when to set boundaries and limits, especially with friends and family.

Mixed: Inconsistent and odd, people with mixed hands are most unhappy when they try to stuff themselves into a category or role that just doesn't work out for the long run. Don't beat yourself up if you can't apply yourself to the same career or relationship for decades at a time. Instead, embrace the fact that you can handle many diverse projects and friendships at one time or in succession. Allow your ability to mix and mingle with many different types of personalities to bring people and ideas together.

Earth: Suspicious, critical, impatient, and temperamental, people with earth hands get easily frustrated when overwhelmed by a cluttered, busy, or impractical person or environment. People with earth hands need to carve out personal space if they have an especially stressful job or live with a messy roommate.

Air: Immature and constantly torn between intuition and facts, people with air hands may be perceived as oddballs. People with air hands need mental stimulation and aren't suited to jobs or romantic relationships that don't give their brains a run for their money.

Fire: Impatient, changeable, and impulsive, fire people may exasperate their parents and bosses who just want them to settle down and do their job consistently. Fire-handed people have to keep themselves busy in constructive ways. Otherwise, they'll get annoyed and quit all their obligations.

Water: Emotional, sensitive, impressionable, and changeable, water people may look calm on the outside, but inside they are often falling apart with mental issues. People with water hands have to find ways to manage stress so they won't worry so much about other people and things they can't change.

Weak fingers

If your first phalange is significantly short, you may find that you are insensitive or not very observant. It's not a pleasant trait to have in a marriage, but it's good if you want to take on a job that involves high emotions that might burn out other types of people. If your middle phalange is shorter than the first, scholarly pursuits may end in frustration and low grades in some educational contexts. However, there are jobs that require great instincts and hard work that don't require a high level of education. If your base phalange is shorter than either of the others, you'll find that physical activity is hard for you, so don't take on a job as a day laborer. Instead, find ways to put your mind to work.

A short or skinny thumb shows that patience, unconditional love, and willpower are not your strong points. This may make parenting or dealing with kids who aren't your own very frustrating, with which you will need regular help. However, you may be able to help others set healthy boundaries for themselves since you don't tolerate a lot of wasted time and energy. If your thumb is set very high on the palm, you are very specialized in your skills and will not do as well in jobs or situations that force you to apply your intelligence to an oversized range of activities. If your thumb is set very low on the hand, you may be overly cautious and unable to take risks, so choose financial and relationship investments that don't require too much of a leap of faith.

Shorter Jupiter fingers, ending well below the nail of Saturn, can indicate a follower. Caution needs to be taken not to fall into a bad relationship or addiction. Help yourself by only keeping good company and cutting yourself off from bad influences. Don't be afraid to reach out for professional help when you see yourself caught in a problem you can't solve on your own. An excessively small angle or gap between the Jupiter finger and your middle finger indicates that you have a hard time being alone. Don't let your need for others cause you to have rebound relationships. If that angle is excessively large, you may need your personal space, so don't move in with a new lover too quickly, or take a job that forces you to work too closely with others.

You can consider your Saturn finger short if the bordering two fingers equal its length. In the case of the short Saturn finger, you might feel a lack of direction in life. Your own sense of passion and drive can falter at times, leading to the danger of latching on to an overbearing person who seems to have a purpose. If you have a short Saturn finger, make sure that you are independent emotionally and financially, and understand that you may have to push yourself instead of finding the natural passion that seems to make life easy for other people. If your Saturn is skinny or has large gaps between it and the surrounding fingers, this is an "isolated Saturn," indicating a loner. Don't force yourself to work as part of a team, or chide yourself if your relationships are not as close as the ones on television.

A short Apollo finger means that you may not understand a lot of forms of artistic expression and thus may have trouble relating to the types of people who rant and rave about music or dance. On the flip side, you'll get along better with those who don't make a big deal about home decorating and fashion. An incredibly long Apollo finger isn't so great either, because it means you are an attention-seeker and risk-taker. You'll have to find appropriate ways to put yourself in the spotlight without causing drama for your loved ones and everyone who has to work with you.

A short Mercury finger indicates somebody who is not too quick with numbers, words, or driven to succeed in business deals. This person deserves a partner who likes the strong, silent type, and a down-to-earth, straightforward job. If your Mercury finger is bent, not just leaning but crooked, it means that you might have trouble with honesty or tact. Perhaps you tend to bend the truth to suit your needs, or you might be so brash that you exaggerate or hurt peoples' feelings. A bent Mercury finger requires that you think before speaking or writing, and fact-check yourself before releasing information.

Weak lines

Earlier in this book I described how you can work toward lengthening or deepening lines in your hands. The process of changing lines can take years, and you may easily encounter frustration if features don't seem to change quickly enough. Some aspects of lines are more fixed than their depth and length, and we will explore those in this chapter.

A simian crease is when the head and heart lines appear to be joined as one, single line. Some palmists believed at one point that it was a sign of low intelligence, as it is often present on the hands of people with Down's syndrome. However, it is also present on the hands of people with high intelligence who have no chromosomal abnormality at all; it merely represents a single-mindedness that can cause others to underestimate intelligence. If you have a simian crease, it will be frustrating if you put yourself in a position where you have to be the master of many intellectual tasks or disciplines. Instead, allow yourself to specialize and cut yourself some slack. You aren't bad at the other things on which you can't seem to focus; you just have a different kind of "smart" that is well applied to your chosen devotions.

A straight or extremely short heart line is rare, since there is usually at least one rise or dip and some degree of length, but it can indicate the person may have trouble relating to those who are more flowery and emotional. Someone with a straight heart line does not do well in relationships or jobs that attempt to provoke an emotional response he or she just can't provide. Instead, this kind of person should find people who appreciate his or her emotional even keel and want a stable rock instead of a sensitive poet. If your heart line has an extreme number of branches, you may have a hard time being selective and discriminating with your lovers. Such a person may not ever be suited to rigid monogamy; forcing yourself into that type of relationship can lead to broken hearts and frustration.

As was mentioned in the section on positive aspects of the head line in this chapter, often the head and life lines cross, which is a good thing. However, there is nearly always a conflict or a challenge in life when such crosses occur, even if the head line starts inside the life line and then crosses to escape it. Many times, this happens early on and simply represents an illness or injury in childhood you have already resolved. If such crosses happen later in life, however, they can represent a crisis mental or physical in nature. Perhaps a midlife crisis or a mental breakdown has or will occur when the cross happens. For some people, this cross represents coming to terms with family issues from the past such as an adoption or childhood abuse. Recognize that you may need counseling or other support, and make sure that you don't make rash decisions during your period of challenge—and end up divorced multiple times, owning several sports cars!

You don't have to worry about a short life line, as people who are concerned about this aren't familiar with palmistry. As you well know, length can vary over the course of your existence. However, if your life line is very angular, and seems to wander in a jerky manner around your palm rather than making a smooth arc, it can indicate that your life takes an erratic course. Either you don't adapt well to change, or you force change on yourself because you haven't found your moorings. Evaluate whether you are the type of person who sabotages jobs and relationships just to make a change. Find another outlet for your need for excitement. If, on the contrary, you fall apart whenever life doesn't seem to be going your way, consider what resources you can use to strengthen your adaptability and flexibility in the face of change. Plan ahead and take full advantage of offers to help you move, care for a newborn baby, or transition to a new position at your work. Simply taking a leap of faith and seeing if you can go with the flow this time is not the right course of action for you—it will only end in tears and disaster.

If other lines on the hand are weak—including the destiny line, rising line to Apollo, rising line to Jupiter, and rising line to Mercury—keep in mind that these lines change more easily because they are more likely to be faint and free-floating rather than attached to an edge of the hand. So take heart, and mind the advice written previously in this book if you'd like to see the rest of your lines become longer, more solid, or deeper.

Are there faulty fingerprints?

Some people have an easier time of life than others, and if you have a lot of bull's-eye shaped whorls on your fingertips, you may have a lot of work to do in the areas of life that those fingers represent. Read more about how karma relates to your dermatoglyphs in the following section on using palmistry for spiritual purposes. As I wrote earlier, usually more whorls on the palm is a good thing, although of course sometimes your strengths can also be your weaknesses. A mark of royalty may mean that you give too much to your family, a mark of humor can mean that you make cruel jokes, and a whorl on Uranus may cause you to be a bit too eccentric.

There are a few loop-type whorls that can be problematic. The loop of ego is a loop-style whorl that can have negative consequences if its effects are unchecked. The loop of ego begins at the junction of the ring finger and pinkie finger, and then swirls across the Apollo mount. It indicates a sense of self-importance and entitlement that can lead to hurt feelings. Actively serving others who are less fortunate as a volunteer can serve to give a bit of perspective to those with a loop of ego and lessen its negative qualities. The loop of response, on the mount of Venus along the edge of the hand (not to be mistaken for the loop of music at the base of the mount of Venus), gives a person an incredible sense of empathy. Unfortunately, the loop of response can be a hard personality trait with which to deal, because it forces a person to take on the moods of his or her surroundings. People with a loop of response may need to take care to surround themselves only with positive people and influences to avoid depression. The humanitarian loop, found running vertically alongside the life line and destiny line in the center of the palm, can also cause difficulty. It means you're a good person, but you may find yourself continuously discouraged and disillusioned by the society you're drawn to serve. Strong hand characteristics can make this loop beneficial, as can an attitude detached from outcomes.

However, the only whorl that is almost universally a bad thing is a whorl on the mount of Neptune, which is located on the interior edge of your lunar mount. Think of this whorl as a whirlpool of self-destructive energy that can suck you too deep into the waters of your mental turmoil. If you see a whorl on Neptune, you'll need to reach out for help when you face your dark side, and it may represent a lifetime of managing mental illness or emotional unrest. A whorl on Neptune doesn't have to indicate madness, just that you are your own worst enemy. But when a whorl in Neptune is combined with other palmistry aspects like, say, a head line swooping deep into your lunar mount representing your psyche, pointed fingertips indicating a sensitive nature, and small thumbs indicating trouble with willpower, you would have to work on changing those more flexible aspects of yourself in order to mitigate the effects of the whorl on Neptune.

Remember always that the unchanging parts of palmistry don't mean that you're doomed, simply that you are now empowered with the framework of your limitations. Knowing yourself means that you actually have the freedom to stop hitting your head against a wall of things you can't change, and instead work with your strengths. We all have weaknesses and potentials. The difference between the empowered palmistry expert and the fool in denial is the ability to make smart choices to maximize the desired potential.

Using palmistry in a spiritual context

What does palmistry have to do with spirituality? Chiromancy, along with all other forms of divination, is inherently spiritual because it suggests a source of wisdom beyond normal, everyday knowledge. Whether you believe the answers that lie in palmistry come from your higher self within expressing your own inner wisdom through your hands, or whether you believe that a god, goddess, or group of deities wrote your destiny in your palms before birth, this section aims to aid you in your spiritual quest on earth using palmistry.

In many religions, hands have been identified as important spiritual centers of the body. Those who study chakras—wells of energy that occur within the body—identify a small center of energy in the palm of each hand through which energy exits or enters the body. Hands-on healing has been a part of the human experience since prehistory, due to the observation of both the sensitivity hands have and the aid hands can administer. Some religions include mudras, sacred hand positions used during prayer.

Mudras for prayers and blessings to create change

The classic palms-together prayer position seen in Christianity, Buddhism, Hinduism, and other religions is quite meaningful in the context of palmistry. When you hold your hands in this position during prayer, you'll notice that you enclose the destiny that lies in your palms between your two hands, as if in sacred offering, and your thumbs point toward your head or your heart depending on where you hold your hands. Remember that your thumbs represent your will or the force of your desire. Depending on your prayers, be mindful of how you hold your hands. If you are praying to worship divinity, consider holding your hands so that your thumbs point toward your chest, the center of your devotion and the resting place of your heart. If you are praying to honor ancestors and teachers or to change your habits of mind, hold your hands higher so that your thumb points toward your head, the center of your thought.

An ancient Greek Pagan blessing made with the hand, especially before an important speech, was to hold out the first three fingers. To make a sign of blessing, hold up the thumb to invoke increase, the pointer finger for fortunate guidance, and the middle finger for rain (since Saturn was also the domain of weather in their palmistry system). Another Pagan blessing, of the Horned God of the Witches, was said to be the pointer finger and pinkie finger held upright, in the manner you might see at rock concerts. The polarity of the Jupiter finger's forthrightness and the trickster nature of Mercury are indicated with the blessing.

Mudras for meditation to create change

The prayer and blessing mudras described in this book are believed to bring about spiritual change via a connection with divinity flowing through a person and through the hands. Another way of thinking of this energy flow (with or without a belief in higher powers) is through energy flow during meditation. Eastern philosophy holds that when life energy is not freely flowing, if it slows or gets stuck inside the body, ill health and spiritual unrest will be a consequence. Since the hands are powerful energy centers that display their meanings through palmistry, you can hold your hands in specific mudra positions while sitting quietly in meditation in order to open up and encourage necessary energy flow. You might recognize many of the mudras described below from Indian art, as India is a source of both mudras and palmistry methods.

Detox mudra: Holding your palm up, lay your thumb across your palm to point directly at your ring finger. Since your Apollo finger is associated with healing, this mudra is practiced to direct negative or toxic energy with the spiritual will of your thumb out of your ring fingertip.

Jnana mudra: With palms up, touch your thumbs and pointer fingers together lightly, with the hands otherwise relaxed. The will of the spirit represented by the thumb touched to the sense of self represented by the Jupiter finger is meant to open you up to be receptive during meditation to spiritual evolution or psychic intuition.

Jupiter mudra: This mudra is to be used when you feel out of control of your life, in order to take charge of your destiny by using the energy released from your Jupiter fingers. Lace the fingers of your hands clasped together, and then let your pointer fingers touch each other and your thumbs touch each other. Relax this pose in your lap during seated meditation and contemplate your power.

Kubera mudra: This mudra is used to invite abundance, whether in the form of material wealth or simply confidence that you have everything you need. Holding your palm upward, lay your ring finger across your palm and then touch your thumb, pointer finger and middle finger together, allowing your pinkie finger to relax freely. This draws energy from your triangle of earnings and directs it out through the fingers associated with your initiative, hard work, and willpower to draw richness into your life.

Inner self mudra: Touching the bases of your wrists together, create as many points of contact as you can between your two thumbs and your two pinkie fingers. Make sure the other three fingers are touching their respective partners. This mudra circulates energy from your higher self back into your inner sense of wisdom, creating a force-feedback loop that promotes awareness of your subconscious and intuition.

Lotus mudra: Meant to look like the flower, this mudra is created by holding the bases of your palms together and creating as many points of contact as you can between your two thumbs and your two pinkie fingers while curling the other fingers away in a bloomlike manner. Since your Mercury finger is associated with communication and your thumb with spiritual will, this mudra is intended to invite love and compassion into your life.

Prithvi mudra: Holding your palm vertically, curl your ring finger downward and hold it with your thumb. Since the Apollo finger is associated with healing, this gesture is intended to be healing for emotional balance by circulating energy out through the Apollo finger and into your thumb. You may notice a body temperature change when this mudra is used in meditation.

Saturn mudra: This mudra is used to balance your conscious mind with your subconscious. It is particularly useful in seated meditation if you find yourself being self-destructive or sabotaging things in your life unwittingly. Palms facing upwards, touch the middle finger of the hand to the center of its palm. Hold it in place with your thumb so you can keep each hand in this position.

A field guide to the spiritual person's hand

An angle in the head line, particularly a diagonal head line or a steep kink (though even a branch at an angle will do), represents a conversion to a new religious faith, an initiation, or a sense of being reborn into a new spiritual awareness. In the case of people who have a yin yang symbol as a fingerprint, the faith connection may be to an Eastern religion. People who have a double life line, or sister line, are spiritually protected by the extra wells of energy contained in the sister line. Think of the sister line as a conscience, the angel on your shoulder, or the extra sense of moral integrity that can keep you from winding up in serious trouble with spirit.

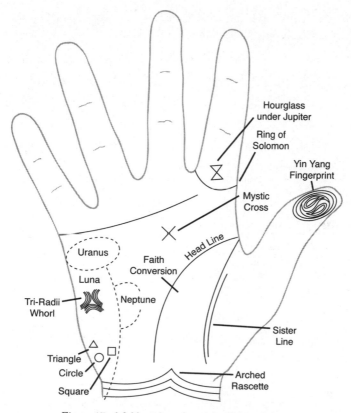

Figure 17: A field guide to the spiritual person's hand

Some other signs of spirituality are a mystic cross, indicating a degree of proficiency in the occult, and a ring of Solomon, showing psychic intuition as well as a call to service of humanity, which are both considered excellent spiritual traits in many religious faith traditions. An intuition line can indicate a psychic or a spiritual healer. A top rascette arching high into the palm, especially on a woman, may indicate a person whose spiritual vocation must supersede a family life.

Pay special attention to the whole percussive side of the hand, since those mounts of Luna, Neptune, and Uranus can all relate directly to spirituality, and the presence of a tri-radii whorl pattern can indicate psychic strength when found on any of these. Squares, triangles, an hourglass under Jupiter, and whorls are all signs of karma, which we will discuss next.

Karma

The concept of karma is closely tied to faith traditions that include reincarnation. Reincarnation is the belief that after death, one's soul is reborn into a new body. There are two views on karma important keep in mind within palmistry's context: the Eastern notion of karma associated with Hindu and Buddhist traditions, and the New Age or Western idea of karma. The reason that both the Western and Eastern views of karma are found in palmistry is that chiromancy evolved independently in many cultures, including those with both karmic faith traditions, and modern palmistry draws from many sources so it includes both. As you read the descriptions of karma, you can decide which understanding of karma best fits your personal belief system and work only with that, or you can use both understandings to further your spiritual growth.

The Eastern idea of karma is that karma is comprised of the desires for and consequences of actions that attach to you over a lifetime. For example, when you cheat on a lover and hurt that person's feelings, you gain karma. When you become president of the country and help many people while gaining fame and fortune, that is also karma. From the Eastern viewpoint, all forms of karma accumulation are to be avoided, because they attach you to an identity here on earth, which takes you further into the cycle of death and rebirth instead of detaching you from your human identities and desires so you can be entirely with the gods. Ideally, to escape all karma, one should remove desire for an outcome from actions. For example, thinking only of spiritual things while cleaning out the garage, instead of desiring a clean garage or a happy spouse as a result of your actions, is best. Thus, no matter whether or not the garage cleaning task is completed sufficiently, you will not gain karma, but will grow closer to divinity. Some Eastern faith traditions hold that no individual can escape the cycle of death and rebirth until we all do so together, while others believe that any person can achieve this "enlightened" escape within a given lifetime.

The Western view of karma also believes karma to be a consequence of actions, good or bad. However, the bad actions are to be avoided, since they accumulate bad karma, while the good actions are to be performed to gain good karma. In the Western notion of karma, the consequences of good or bad karma are visited upon the practitioner within this lifetime or the next. So if you cheat on a lover and hurt his or her feelings, you may suffer similar betrayal.

If you help other people as president, you will be helped in return. The negative consequences of bad karma act to teach the person a lesson so that, in this life or the next, that particular karmic lesson will not have to be repeated. Believers in the Western notion of karma may or may not also strive to escape the cycle of death and rebirth by completing all necessary lessons as an individual or as a collective society.

Where to find karma in your hand

An hourglass under the pointer finger, on the mount of Jupiter, has already been mentioned earlier in this book as a sign of good karma payback. Of course, this sign is most positive if you subscribe to the Western view that collecting good karma is a spiritual mission in life.

Some palmistry experts believe that because you're born with the same fingerprints, which you will keep over your lifetime, your fingerprints mark a record of the karmic strengths and weaknesses you've been given to work with. Bull's-eyes, and to a lesser extent ovals, show where your karma is negative or has accumulated, or where you need to focus spiritually during this life. Bull's-eyes aren't a bad thing, even if you subscribe to the Eastern theory of karma. They just show you where your focus should lie, and even where you've already done a lot of work to earn blessings. In fact, any whorls lend you the strength to know yourself. Loops and tents show a work in progress during this lifetime, including lessons or a reduction of attachments that will unfold in their own time as well as those through which you are progressing nicely.

Remember that fingerprints don't change over this lifetime, so even if you complete a karmic lesson or rid yourself of a karmic attachment, you will still wear that whorl like a badge of honor for that battle. But who knows—maybe in your next life you'll be born as a person with a different fingerprint pattern due to the achievements you've made during this lifetime. As of yet, we have no way to prove or disprove reincarnation, so it is up to you whether or not to consider karma as part of your spiritual practice.

For markings that can change over this lifetime, although they may also stick around as a badge of honor, include the powerhouse for karmic work that is the sister line to the life line, and those small shape markings such as triangles. Squares can represent reserves of energy on hand when you're ready to get through a karmic advancement, while triangles are an extra boost showing dynamic progress.

No matter why you think we are here on earth, you can integrate palmistry into your daily prayer or devotional practice. Pray with your hands in a mudra meaningful to you, such as palms together, and ask your higher self or your chosen deity or deities to guide your life and help you with karma. Then open your hands and take a look. Your answers from the divine are right in front of your face.

Five

READING
FOR OTHERS

By now, you already have a wealth of palmistry information at your fingertips that can be applied to others just as easily as to yourself. You may have already taken a peek at the palm of somebody close to you while reading this book—that's a wonderful start! But remember that palmistry is more than a parlor trick; the true strength I hope for you to discover in this book is how your hands can change over time. When you do palmistry readings for others, be sure to impress upon them that their reading is just a snapshot of a potential destiny. You may even wish to share with somebody close to you the changes that you've seen in your own hands and life. Ideally, if you can get a family member or friend to agree to keep a palmistry journal too, you'll both have maps of your lives in your hands that you can compare and contrast.

First, some ground rules. Try your best never to read aloud somebody's palm without their permission. At best, delivering fortune-telling of any kind unbidden can be perceived as rude, and at worst it can scare people away from the noble art of chiromancy if you grab their hand and start talking about bad news, or if you start piping up with unwanted advice. It may feel weird the first time you ask somebody if you can read their palm, especially if you're new at this and may have to be leaning over this book the entire time. Approach a friend or family member, book in hand, and ask if they can help you try out what you've learned in this book. It can be a fun experiment for both of you.

The way a person holds out their hand to you is an interesting aspect you can't try on yourself, and a good way to make sure that the person is ready for a palm reading. Sometimes the way the person holds their hand may change during a reading, so take notice of that as well. For example, a hand may be held out at first with fingers spread wide, and then slowly the fingers will draw closer together as the reading progresses. This should trigger you to ask if there are any questions or concerns, and to verify whether it is okay to proceed with the reading.

The fan: Fingers spread wide and hand tilted back on the wrist. The person who displays their hand like a fan is ready, open, and willing to have a palm reading. Relax and tell this person what they needs to hear. Advice will be willingly considered.

The natural: A relaxed hand, held out without any tension in the fingers or palm, is a good sign that someone is ready for a reading. Trusting and unstressed, such a person may or may not believe your reading, but it won't be cause for fear or upset.

The paddle: Fingers close together and muscles a bit tense, the paddle hand indicates that this person may not trust you entirely yet. This may be a first date, or somebody who is new to you or palm reading in general. A paddle hand is cause for you to perhaps ask again if this person is sure about wanting a reading. If so, it is okay to proceed, but know that your advice may fall on deaf ears.

The claw: Fingers are hooked, tense, and spread wide while the palm is also tense and cupped. The person who displays a claw hand to you may think this is a big joke, or may be eager to trick you or take something from this reading that is not entirely positive. If somebody shows you the claw hand, you may want to stop this reading for now and say "maybe later."

Anatomy of a good lover: reading the palm of your spouse, significant other, or date

It might feel awkward to ask to perform a palm reading on a first date, but it can be a really flirty move and great icebreaker. Not only will you make this date one to remember, but hey, look, you're holding hands already and you didn't even have to be sneaky about it. After asking your date about any plans for the future is a great time to sneak in a palm reading. "I would love to try to tell your fortune! Are you right- or left-handed?" Ask for the person to hold out the nondominant hand so you can see what love destiny the passive hand has to share, and you're on your way. Don't forget to thank your date for being a good sport and trying out your palmistry skills after the reading, and give that hand a flirty squeeze before you let go! A quick joke about how now that you know his or her future, you'd love to hear more about his or her past will diffuse any nervousness and keep the conversation going.

You can look for some exciting signs on a lover right away, like the stuff you already saw on your palm in the section about focusing your palm reading on love. For example, a destiny line or rising line of Saturn through the lunar mount indicates someone who is good marriage material. But the true strength of reading your beloved's palms as they change is in looking for comparisons. After all, you know now that palmistry is an art best practiced frequently, and so it isn't as useful just to take a look at your lover's palm and see good things. After all, since palm features change every day, whatever good you see may not apply to what the two of you have or don't have together tomorrow. However, if you look at that snapshot of his or her palm today and compare it to your palm today, you'll be seeing a full picture of what your relationship or budding romance truly is right now. Comparing palm readings is like seeing a visual representation of how your energies are interacting with each other, seeing your shared destiny unfolding in 3D.

Put your finger on your relationship

First, compare your thumbs to one another. Ideally, the two of you will have an equal strength of will for a harmonious relationship, so one person's thumb should not be way more bulbous and fat than the other's. If one person does have a more delicate and tiny thumb, an average-sized thumb is a suitable match. If you find yourselves with mismatched thumbs, you'll have to work out an agreeable power dynamic between the two of you in order not to have big, blow-out fights all the time.

Remember to check the base of the thumb for the mount of Venus and compare each other's love meter. The fullness and vivid color of Venus represents your capacities for love. If you have a large and red Venus and your lover has a deflated and pale Venus, you may often feel that your affections are not returned. It isn't that your mate doesn't love you, just that your capacities to give love and your appetite for affection are different. If your Venus mounts are mismatched, the one with the lower love drive will have to find a fulfilling way to express love, or the one with the higher love drive may need to seek additional affection elsewhere.

While examining the mount of Venus, compare the amount of worry lines radiating out from the base of the thumb. Ideally, the two of you should be sharing the burden of the natural anxieties that arise in a relationship and in a shared life. However, if one partner is doing all the worrying for the two of you, it may be a clue about how to improve your relationship. Of course, it's perfectly natural for one partner to worry more than the other, but it can be easy for too much responsibility to shift gradually. The partner who is less of a worrywart should step in to help out with some more of the financial, household, or parenting needs of the couple.

Your other fingers hold important clues to the compatibility between your minds. Look to the second phalanges on both peoples' hands. The second phalange is the middle segment of each finger, just between the knuckles. If your second phalanges are relatively long, indicating an intellectual streak, and your lover's second phalanges are short, indicating somebody more interested in the physical and instinctual than matters of the mind, you won't find much common ground in conversation.

Check out your fingertips to compare sensitivity levels to see if you will step on each others' feelings. Pointed or conic fingers have similar levels of sensitivity, as do square or spatulate fingertips. When mismatched, you might find those with the more sensitive pointed or conic fingers feel

like they are being mistreated while those with the spatulate or square fingers feel they've been misunderstood. Sensitivity level matches don't necessarily mean compatibility,
either. Sensitive people paired together can get into cruel
and insensitive arguments, too. Understanding your differences or similarities can make your relationship stronger.

Do your roads to love lead to the same place?
Of course, you'll want to compare heart lines, hoping for balance in a similarity of depth and curve. Deep heart lines indicate more emotional people who wear their hearts on their
sleeves, while shallow or chained heart lines show somebody
with less capacity to cry at everything. Mismatched depth of
heart lines is okay if there is an understanding about each
others' nature regarding emotional expression, but the mismatch can also lead to misinterpretations about feelings.
Similarly, somebody with a straight heart line may be more
practical about love, and if he or she is stuck with a lover
with a curvy heart line, such a lover may have expectations
for love that are too high for him or her.

Where do your heart lines end? In the case of the ter-
mination of the heart line, you don't necessarily need or
want them to end in the same place. As you read earlier, in
the section on focusing your palm readings on love, where
your heart line ends indicates the way in which you love
and, to some extent, the type of person to whom you are
attracted. Look at the finger to which each of your heart

lines point and think about how well you match the qualities of that finger.

For example, if your lover has a heart line that terminates at Saturn, showing a need for a traditional relationship with a level-headed, responsible person, hopefully you're not a professional body-painting artist who values free love. If your lover's heart line ends at Jupiter and you're a clingy person, he or she may long for somebody with more of a sense of independence. If your heart line indicates an ideal that your lover can't possibly fulfill, or your lover's heart line shows expectations that you know you can't meet, it is important to note before you get wrapped up in a relationship that could lead to disappointment.

Comparing each others' hands for the presence or absence of a girdle of Venus and via lascivia can go a long way toward avoiding frustration. If one of you has either, hopefully your lover will have one or the other as well. If one partner has a girdle of Venus and the other does not, living together may turn out to be irritating to both, since one has a need for beauty and sensuality that may seem shallow or impossible for the other to fulfill. If one lover has a via lascivia and the other does not, your sex drives will be mismatched, and the lover with the via lascivia may find better sexual compatibility with people outside the relationship.

A final word about compatibility: you don't have to find one perfect fit for you, or somebody with twin hands, to find your twin soul. Not every relationship has traditional power dynamics, monogamy, or living situations. Sometimes we even pick people who rub us the wrong way in order to teach us and to soften our own rough edges. So, if you are already married to somebody who isn't a palmistry match, you need not lament. Though a compatibility mismatch can be a red flag marking the issues that need your attention and caution, the purpose of a compatibility reading should be to advise you, rather than to stamp your relationship with a grade. As you learn to compromise, you may find that your hand features begin to change to more resemble one another's.

Reading the palms of your family members

While you can pick your boyfriend, girlfriend, or spouse, you can't pick your family. So, while palmistry comparisons may be frustrating, they can also inform the ways in which you tolerate or understand your family members' choices. Start, please, with your own hand, as discussed in the section earlier in this book on narrowing your palm reading focus to family. After all, the only person you can truly control is yourself, and it's best to begin by understanding how you interact with your family.

Reading your kids' palms

In the past, every important person had an astrological natal chart drawn up at birth, a snapshot of the sky to tell the baby's destiny. Now you have the power to begin reading your child's palms at birth and watch him or her change as time goes on. Making hand prints every year is a common practice with added meaning for those of us into chiromancy. If you start a palmistry journal for each child as a baby, such a special gift can be a cherished heirloom for generations, as well as acting as a welcome parenting aid for you.

A little tip for those of us with babies who want to keep their fists clenched or are always grabbing something: make palm readings into a finger-play game. My one-year-old daughter especially enjoys an old British baby game so old that it is of indeterminate origin. On the flat, open palm of the baby, draw circles with your finger while saying "'Round and 'round the garden, like a teddy bear." Then walk your fingers up the baby's arm, saying "one step, two steps…" and finally tickle the baby under an armpit or chin, saying "Tickle you under there!" My daughter loves to present a palm to me, flat, fingers spread wide, eagerly awaiting a game. While I play with her, I can easily sneak in a palm reading if I perform the game slowly, especially since she loves to play it over and over again many times daily.

We all know that our hands don't resemble the pudgy appendages we had when we were babies, so it is fun to watch the hand shapes, mounts, and lines as they make drastic changes. Individual babies vary significantly, so even though one might imagine that every little doll hand looks alike, relative shapes and lines vary. My own daughter has short fingers, which makes every other baby seem to have long "alien" hands to me. The first few years is the time of life in which you are most likely to be able to observe drastic hand-shape changes, so make a note of the hand-shape category your baby seems to fit, and analyze it again each year. An industrious and messy two-year-old can easily have an elemental hand that morphs slowly into a delicate psychic hand in his or her early teens.

Kids change so quickly, and it's fun to watch their lines crawl around their hands like rivers in different rain seasons. When experiencing frustration with your children, it can be informative to make comparisons between your hands and theirs, similarly to what was done earlier in this chapter with lovers. This time, instead of focusing on the heart line, try comparing your head lines. Comparing head lines can help you determine compatibility with lovers, too, especially as they turn into spouses or life partners and become family!

Check the relative depth of your head line compared to that of your child. If your kid doesn't yet have a deep head line, he or she might not think things through yet. If your line is deeper, you may find yourself frustrated at a perceived lack of attention span or foresight. If your head line is more shallow than that of your kid, you may find your child frustratingly cautious, introverted, and even fearful. A longer or branched head line may show a detail-oriented kid or parent who has a hard time working with a person with a short head line, meaning someone who doesn't sweat the small stuff. Likewise, remember that the relative straightness of the head line indicates practicality. So expect the kid with the wandering head line to have his or her head in the clouds.

Next time you declare thumb war on your school-aged kid, take a moment to compare your strength of will. In the case of the parent-child relationship, you want some disparity in your favor, as opposed to the equality for which one may strive in a romantic partnership. If your child's thumb is thick, long, or bulbous, you know you're up against a strong-willed force of nature. If your own thumb is especially short, thin, and pointed, your level of sensitivity and flexibility may be great in some relationships, but it can be a challenge when parenting.

Reading your mother's palm

In the section on focusing your palmistry reading on a specific topic, you read that your mother is visible on your palm as a mark on the lunar mount. In addition to comparing other aspects of the hand as you do with other people, comparing your lunar mounts can tell you a lot about your relationship with your mother. Even if your lunar mount is not affected in the same way as your mother's, seeing what sort of ideas about motherhood she has had to deal with, and how it translated into who you have become, can be useful information.

For example, whose lunar mount is more full? A robust lunar mount is a sign of a caring and nurturing sense of motherhood. Ideally, your lunar mounts will be of similar constitution, because if your mother showered you with affection, you will pass that on, and if your mom was more of a practical and no-nonsense type, you both may have deflated mounts as a result. However, if there is a big disparity, you may be rebelling against the smothering or detached mothering you received.

Take a look at the coloring as well. There's no such thing as a perfect mom, but if there were, she'd have a uniformly pink lunar mount. More likely, there will be some variation. A red or blotchy lunar mount can indicate some issues deep in the psyche surrounding motherhood, which is actually pretty normal. An extremely pale lunar mount indicates not having enough energy to devote to parenting.

Look for small markings in both hands like squares, circles, ovals, and triangles; these bless your relationship with your mom. Look also for tridents that might represent tough choices, crosses that indicate other relationships which might aid or get in the way of your relationship, and stars that can show a personality clash. These markings can also be present on your father's palm to represent your relationship's trials and joys, most likely near the destiny line.

Reading your father's palm

That rising line to Saturn should be compared on your palm and also on your father's palm. Your destiny line is linked forever with your father, since Saturn's influence and the way you view your dad affects the way you relate to men and authority figures over a lifetime. The destiny line on your dad's hand shows his attitude toward fatherhood, which may have resulted from cultural influences, the way he was raised, and of course fate.

How do the depths of your destiny lines compare? A deep destiny line can indicate a large capacity for a strong relationship, so ideally the depths of your lines will be similar, otherwise the one with the deeper line will be left wanting more of a connection with the other than can be given. A broken destiny line on your dad means there were times in life when he wasn't present, either physically or emotionally. Branching lines from the destiny line can point to other areas of the hand that affect your relationship and beg for a comparison. For example, if a branch points to the head line, you can make a comparison there to see if your ways of thinking are similar, in the same way as you can compare your head line to those of your children as discussed earlier in this chapter.

In some circumstances, one or both of you may have no rising line to Saturn. The absence of a destiny line has a lot to say about your relationship as well, knowing that lines can form and fade as they do. If one of you is missing a destiny line, it means that person has transcended the fatherhood relationship for now (for good or bad), while focusing on other areas of life. Yes, you can form a destiny line, but if your dad is missing one and you feel like you're missing a relationship with him, it may be a good indication that it is not worth your effort to establish one with him.

Reading the palms of siblings, cousins,
and other family generational peers

You already know where the rest of your family members lie on your own palm, and you've gotten a taste of comparing aspects of your hands with your parents, spouse, and kids. Now widen the scope of your study to include comparisons with the palms of your generational peers such as siblings and cousins. Depending on your relationships with them, different lines may be of more interest to you, like the head line if you're having trouble getting on the same wavelength, the destiny line if they're chronically having trouble with money, or the rising line to Mercury if you are having communication problems.

A good place to start is on the area of the palm that represents a relative that you share. For example, if you and your sister share a father, comparing your destiny lines can be interesting, as they show your relationships with your dad, which can have an effect on the way you relate to each other. Have fun, and always remember to tell your relatives that their palm readings can change, even if their family members don't.

Aspects of hands you can
surreptitiously notice on coworkers

In the earlier section on reading your date's palm, I suggested that you always get permission before telling a person's fortune with chiromancy. The same applies doubly to coworkers, since scaring your boss or colleagues with unwanted revelations can be pretty good grounds for getting fired. However, the same problem does not apply if you perform a covert palm reading and keep that knowledge to yourself.

Though some may worry that peeking at another person's destiny without permission is unethical, this information is written on your palms publicly for a reason. Just as we share air that we breathe, it is not wrong to take in psychic knowledge through a palm reading. Just don't go accosting people with that information if they don't feel ready to hear it, since doing so would be a true violation of a person's spiritual will to be in control (or blissfully ignorant) of their destiny.

You may already know the stereotype that a strong handshake represents an assertive person, while a limp handshake represents passivity. Now that you're aware of chiromancy, when you shake anyone's hand you can analyze whether they have a thick and robust hand or a skinny one with slender fingers to instantly figure out the hand-shape type, as well as the smoothness or roughness of the skin to represent their level of sensitivity. If you focus carefully on the handshake, you may even be able to pick up on a mount or two.

For example, let's imagine you're walking into an interview with a potential new boss and she shakes your hand assertively—a good sign. You notice that her hands are thick and a bit rough, so you can imagine that her lack of sensitivity will mean she won't be easily offended, but she may have a hard time noticing your shortcomings and correcting them in a tactful way. You observe that the handshake is tighter closer to your wrist, and that makes you aware of strong muscles that represent a large Jupiter mount. This woman is a born leader, and depending on the type of follower you are, you might work well as her subordinate if you like to be given direction. If you prefer to be treated as a peer, however, you should look elsewhere for a job.

Now, imagine that you interview with another potential boss later in the day who also gives you a strong handshake. His hands are smooth and slender, indicating a perceptiveness the last boss didn't have. You notice that the handshake, though tight overall, squeezes tighter closer to your fingers. This means that, while he has a powerful enough Jupiter mount, his Mercury mount is quite strong as well, allowing him to work as part of a team and communicate well as a leader. Such signs are very good that this boss might be a better manager.

It is very helpful to know whether a boss or coworker means what he or she says when offering you something or asking for your input. Check while he or she is holding a cup of coffee or a pen to see if you can notice whether the Mercury finger is straight or crooked. If straight, you can trust that what is being presenting to you is true at the time, but if that pinkie finger is crooked, you should assume that anything can happen and protect your work and your career accordingly. Likewise, if your colleague tends to keep hands closed in fists when speaking with you, he or she may not be sharing the whole truth.

If you get in an argument with a boss or coworker, you should be able to do a quick thumb comparison, as thumbs are easy to spot. If you're clashing wills with somebody with an especially thick, bulbous, or long thumb, don't expect that person to give in easily, even when wrong. It may be better to try mediation with someone in human resources or in authority, or to use your communication skills to get on the same side rather than to make enemies with such a strong-willed person. Ideally, you should always try to use your palmistry skills to figure out how best to work with others, rather than to dig up dirt on them.

Jewelry and Adornment

Earlier, in the section on using palmistry for spiritual purposes, I discussed how mudras can help energy flow from specific areas of the hand. Energy flow can also be aided purposely by reflexology or acupuncture, but many people unconsciously work to correct problems with energy flow by using jewelry. If you always feel better when wearing a ring on a certain finger, for example, that may be your way of correcting an imbalance in energy flow. Your coworkers may be subtly letting you know things by how they hold objects or wear jewelry. For example, if you know somebody who holds a cigarette or wineglass stem between the middle and ring fingers, this can indicate a desire to impress those around him or her.

If your coworker wears a watch, take note of where the watch is worn. A watch worn on the left wrist can show a traditional or conventional way of working with and dealing with others. If the face of the watch is on the inside of the wrist, however, this may indicate that the person plays as hard as he or she works. A watch worn on the right wrist when a person is left-handed indicates increased intelligence.

Ring location is especially telling if a coworker is wearing a ring on a finger other than the traditional ring finger associated with displaying a wedding ring. Incidentally, the wedding ring is worn on that Apollo finger because it is associated with love relationships and the heart, in the same way that crosses under Apollo display your relationships as lines on your hand. At one point, it was even believed that a vein ran directly from this finger to the heart, which isn't technically true, but is a romantic thought.

Rings on the other fingers enhance the realm in which they have charge. Below is a look at the qualities that might be given to a person wearing a ring on a particular finger. When noticing a ring on another person, you can assume that he or she desires those traits, but may find them a particular challenge naturally.

A ring on the thumb: A person with a ring on the thumb may want healing skills. However, people who have thumb rings may tend to have relationship problems that they hope to rectify.

A ring on the pointer finger: A ring on the pointer finger should draw skill in business and increase power and a sense of honor. In reality, people wearing a ring on this finger may seem controlling, aloof, complaining, and unable to relax without overindulging.

A ring on the middle finger: The person with this ring wants a studious nature and a sense of discipline and reliability. In practice, people wearing this ring may tend to be emotionally flat, depressed, guilty, critical, or lonely.

A ring on the pinkie finger: People may wear a ring here hoping to enhance communication. In practice, a ring worn on the pinkie finger tends to convey a message and show a person who is against conformity and may have trouble being honest, especially in relationships.

Remember that things change in life and with palmistry. That means that a person may have started wearing a ring in a particular location years ago to fix a problem, and now no longer has that problem but still wears the ring out of a sense of familiarity with that particular piece of jewelry. When you do quick and surreptitious readings on other people, always take your discoveries with a grain of salt. After all, you have to spend plenty of time examining and journaling about your own hands to learn their palmistry secrets, so jumping to conclusions about others is not the most accurate way to perform chiromancy.

Working with a palmistry buddy

Reading the palms of others is fun and can be easier to keep up than your own palmistry journal; you'll get positive feedback from an interested person stroking your ego. There's nothing wrong with that, and you can use the joys of reading for others to enhance your palmistry skills. Grab yourself a palmistry buddy, who can be anyone from a co-worker who expressed interest when he saw you reading this book at lunch to your child. Your palmistry buddy can be a best friend who is like a sister to you, or just somebody you met on the Internet who would love to meet up at a café once a week.

Even when you have a palmistry buddy, it's ideal that you both keep your own palmistry journals. Bring your journals with you whenever you meet up and trade them so that your buddy can add his or her drawings and notes on your hand to your journal. Sometimes another person can see changes more easily because he or she doesn't look at your hands every day. A creeping lengthening of the heart line, for example, or a slight puffiness of the hands might be something you'd overlook on yourself quite easily.

The most fun thing to do with a palmistry buddy is to choose a focus, and have him or her read your palm on that topic while striving not to give any feedback until the end of the reading. The reason for this is that you can easily become biased about yourself when life doesn't go the way you want. For example, if you really want to be able to fulfill all the needs of a clingy girlfriend, you might decide that your heart line isn't all that shallow and your mount of Venus not all that deflated, while a palmistry buddy can easily spot the fact that your heart line is more faint than most and your mount of Venus is flat as a pancake. Don't get disheartened if your palmistry buddy doesn't tell you what you want to hear. Remember that the point of the reading is to learn what you can change in your hands and in your life. A desire to act on advice, even if it is tough advice to hear, is why you should try not to smile and nod or look gloomy during your reading. Your palmistry buddy probably wants you to feel good about your time together, and so you might unintentionally steer the reading away from necessary advice if you obviously only want to hear about things that are going well.

Giving a palmistry reading as a gift

A palmistry reading is a wonderful gift for a birthday, bridal shower, wedding, New Year's party, Halloween party, Valentine's Day date, other holiday, baby shower, or baby welcoming party. Consider giving a gift box with a copy of this book, a piece of quality paper rolled up with a ribbon, an ink pad, and a note inviting the person to make a hand-print and give it to you for a free palm reading. If there's a party, have the person make a handprint right there and then. You can write your own notes on the paper in your best handwriting and return it in a scrapbook or binder to help the person start a palmistry journal, or in a frame for display as a work of art.

CONCLUSION

The famous "Serenity Prayer" goes, "God grant me the serenity to accept the things I cannot change, strength to change the things I can, and the wisdom to know the difference." Palmistry gives you the power to begin working on all three parts of that blessing. You have my thanks for giving everyday palmistry a chance. It takes a brave soul to look past the classic stereotype of the back alley palmist who is keen to reveal terrifying information about your future. Luckily, the bold are rewarded with a way to smash the stereotypes by watching real change appear in their own hands, using information within every person's reach. Far from being frightening or limiting, palmistry unleashes the potential within us all.

Hopefully you can see chiromancy's amazing benefits. Everyone carries their palmistry tools in their hands everywhere they go, unlike with other forms of divination. And those tools can be used to answer nearly every question one might have in life. Far from being a recipe for doom written in stone, palmistry readings are more like snapshots of a GPS map of life as you move along your route and make choices. Remember that the future is always changing, and the way it changes is largely in your hands—literally and figuratively!

In order to enjoy the full accuracy and empowerment offered by palmistry, you'll need to commit yourself to checking in with your palms on a frequent basis to notice aspects that change over the course of years, months, days, or even hours. You are a research scientist, and you are your own best subject. The discoveries you make could change the course of your life, and perhaps even change the future of palmistry forever. Just like any serious spiritual discipline, you should take baby steps, but start as soon as possible and keep up the work without ceasing. Get started right away by checking signs on your palms every morning and night. At first, it may feel like a burden to have to lug out a book and remember to check your hands, but you'll soon get used to it so that it will feel like second nature, sort of like glancing at your watch for the time. You'll be glad you kept up with your chiromancy frequently and consistently when a warning or exciting blessing shows up in your palm and leads you to quickly change your course for a more enjoyable day.

Augment your existing prayers, meditations, or devotions. Give yourself a great spiritual gift by setting aside regular personal time to create a palmistry journal and to reflect on the resulting wisdom. Not only will you discover differences you might not have otherwise noticed, but you will empower yourself with evidence of the result of your efforts to be in charge of your own destiny. Your self-improvements are limited only by your desire and sincere efforts, since you are now able to examine your personality strengths and weaknesses, to focus on important topics like love and career in order to change your future, and even to bless others with the insights offered by palmistry. The power is in your hands to change your life outlook, both outside and inside yourself.

Remember that whenever you offer a palmistry reading to another, you are an ambassador for the ancient art of chiromancy. You will naturally want to make sure that your participants have a good time and benefit from the amazing discoveries and confirmations written in their own hands. However, you also have the responsibility to dispel myths that palmistry can predict when people die or that a palm reading is a parlor trick only worth trying once in a lifetime. So go ahead and give your friend a hand with palmistry, but give him or her a piece of your mind as well.

As you use the map of life in your palms to walk your journey, share your story. Whenever you impart a reading, include a little tidbit somebody might notice changing in their own hands, like a cross of relationships appearing under Apollo, child lines manifesting on the Mercury mount, or a red dot on the Jupiter mount that can appear in an instant to warn of an oncoming migraine and disappear after the headache has subsided. Even a skeptic will enjoy information about verifiable changes that stick in his or her mind, and who knows—maybe you'll be thanked at a later time. We can all help this ancient art endure and thrive in our modern world by expanding the use of palmistry to the everyday.

GLOSSARY

Active hand: Your dominant hand. The one you usually use to write or catch a ball.

Active Mars: A mount between the thumb and life line, above the Venus mount. This is how you express yourself assertively to the world. It holds keys to your temper and hostility. This area is also sometimes associated with the god Vulcan and called "the area of family aggression."

Adversity lines: Curving lines that begin at the thumb edge of the hand and curve steeply up through the mount of Venus. Each line can be said to represent a significant enemy or opponent in our lives that challenge us with conflict.

Air: A hand shape associated with a square palm with long fingers. People with air hands are thoughtful, innovative, intuitive, and intellectual.

Apollo finger: Your ring finger, having to do with creative expression and exchange, especially in the arts.

Apollo mount: The fleshy lump below your ring finger. *See* Apollo finger.

Apollo rising line: A vertical line from the bottom of the palm pointing up toward the ring finger is your rising line to Apollo, indicating successful artistic endeavors.

Athena: The middle or second phalange of the thumb, associated with logic.

Broken line: A line with many breaks in it indicates a disruption in or disappearance of energy associated with that line during a period of time in life.

Butterfly: A large horizontal hourglass found in the center of the palm, with one edge on the life line. The sign of the butterfly marks somebody as a playful free spirit and an excellent friend.

Chaining: Islands found within a line can indicate weakened energy, except in the case of the family chain.

Chiromancy: *See* palmistry.

Conic: A hand shape that is generally wider at the base than the fingers with long fingers that may or may not be coned or pointed. Skin is smooth and hands appear soft, light, and graceful. Lines may be numerous and wandering. People with conic hands are artistic, daring, passionate, sensitive, and intuitive. Conic hands are associated with the signs of Cancer and Libra.

Cross: In general, crosses are good things, and they indicate a focus of positive energy or a good meeting or relationship with another person.

Cross of mystery: *See* mystic cross.

Dermatoglyphics: The study of the meanings of fingerprints.

Destiny line: The same thing as a rising line of Saturn. *See also* rising line and Saturn finger.

Digit: A finger or thumb.

Divination: A system of rules and interpretations for fortune-telling, often involving tools.

Domain: A realm or area in which a ruler holds control; in the context of palmistry, each part of the palm rules over a specific aspect of life.

Earth: A hand shape that consists of a square palm with short fingers. Lines are usually deep but few in number. Those with earth hands are practical, reliable, healthy, and stable.

Elementary: A hand shape that is generally large with blunt features and short fingers. Fingernails are wide and square. Skin has a rough texture, and lines are generally straight, short, and shallow. People with elementary hands often love nature, and are hard-working and stubborn. Elementary hands are associated with the sign of Taurus and the element of earth.

Energy: Unlike the scientific term, in this book "energy" is used as a word for the life essence that flows through all things and animates the universe.

Escape lines: Horizontal lines that begin on the percussive edge of the hand and travel across the mount of Luna, these show somebody with the urge to move away from problems. Sometimes called "travel lines," these are not positive signs like relocation lines on the life line, but can represent escape through substance abuse.

Family chain: A chained line at the base of the thumb. The more chained this line, the stronger the emotional ties with one's family. The nature of this line, whether thinning or breaking, can also show family separation or emotional detachment.

Fire: A hand shape consisting of a long rectangular or oval palm with short fingers. Fire-handed people are temperamental and impatient, but very energetic and versatile.

Fortune-telling: Spiritually discovering personality characteristics, and also the past, present, and especially the future.

Girdle of Venus: A curving horizontal line from around the pointer finger to the pinkie finger that shows sensual joys, both sexual and for the pleasures of beauty and good taste in all their forms.

Grille: Also called a grid, a grille is a hash mark on the palm made of multiple small horizontal and vertical lines. These indicate a barrier, and can be found along a line or on any mount or finger. A more subtle block can also be found on a line, as a small tick mark or a bar.

Head line: The middle major horizontal line on your hand, this line has to do with your mind, your way of thinking about the world, and the intellectual aspects of your personality.

Heart line: The top of the three major horizontal lines of the hand, having to do with your emotions, love life, and journey through connecting with a soulmate.

Hepatica: Health line, also known as the rising line to Mercury.

Humanitarian loop: A loop running vertically, parallel to the life line and destiny line, in the center of the palm, indicating a person drawn to hope for the best in society and to serve humanity.

Intuition: Understanding the present, past, or future using a knowledge source from within, rather than the five senses.

Intuition line: A line beginning on the mount of Luna on the percussive edge of the hand and sweeping upward through the lunar mount. If it points to the head line, it indicates a natural healer, and if it points to the destiny line, it indicate a natural psychic.

Islands: *See* chaining.

Jupiter finger: Your pointer finger, having to do with leadership, your own authority, strength of personality, and goal-oriented nature.

Jupiter mount: The fleshy lump underneath your pointer finger. *See also* Jupiter finger.

Jupiter rising line: A vertical line from the bottom of the palm moving up next to the life line and pointing toward the pointer finger, having to do with your leadership and social roles.

Karma: In its New Age context, karma often means lessons to be learned in this lifetime, as well as the natural spiritual consequences of right and wrong action. In the Eastern context that also applies to palmistry, karma represents your ties to people as you give to and take from them, as well as to earthly things and situations when you are attached emotionally to outcomes you desire.

Life line: The line curving around your thumb and mount of Venus, having to do with your life's path and health. Also called the Venusian line.

Lines: The roads on the map of the hand, the lines show the plot line of your life as it is forming in front of you.

Loop: A type of dermatoglyph that looks like oblong or misshapen concentric circles or ovals. In general, it means variability or flexibility, but there are several specific loop locations that have other meanings.

Loop of common sense: A loop starting at the junction between your middle finger and ring finger, indicating a responsible and thoughtful person.

Loop of courage: A loop on active Mars, at the junction between your thumb and pointer finger under the start of the life line, indicating bravery.

Loop of ego: A loop starting at the junction between your ring finger and pinkie finger, jutting diagonally onto the mount of Apollo. It indicates a sense of entitlement.

Loop of humor: A loop starting at the junction between your ring finger and pinkie finger and jutting down onto the mount of Mercury, indicating an oddball sense of humor. *See also* mark of humor if the dermatoglyph is not a loop.

Loop of inspiration: A loop starting at the base of the palm, sweeping up from the wrist onto the mount of Neptune on the interior edge of the lunar mount, indicating a person who is moved to creative greatness by emotional inspiration.

Loop of memory: A horizontal loop in the center of the palm running parallel to the head line, indicating a fine memory for details.

Loop of music: A loop starting at the base of the palm on the thumb edge of the hand, sweeping upward from the wrist onto the mount of Venus, indicating a talented musician.

Loop of recall: A loop between the heart and head lines, usually under the junction between your ring and pinkie fingers, indicating a person with instant recall for large quantities of information.

Loop of response: A loop starting on the thumb edge of the hand, sweeping onto the mount of Venus, indicating a very empathic person.

Loop of stringed music: A loop in the center of the Venus mount, indicating a special appreciation for music from stringed instruments.

Lunar mount: Located along the percussive edge of your hand, this mount has to do with your inner psyche.

Magic bracelet: Three deep, complete rascettes, indicating safety and health during travel. Lines from these rascettes to the Jupiter finger, Apollo finger, or lunar mount are also good signs for travel associated with fortune, fame, and love respectively.

Mark of humor: A whorl on the palm at the junction of your Apollo and Mercury fingers, indicating a sharp and sometimes caustic wit. *See also* loop of humor if this whorl is a loop-type whorl.

Mark of nobility: A whorl on the palm at the junction of your Saturn and Apollo fingers, indicating a drive to help the defenseless and speak for those who do not have a voice.

Mark of royalty: A whorl on the palm at the junction of your Jupiter and Saturn fingers, representing close family ties and a sense of duty to kin.

Mark of the teacher: Two parallel diagonal lines on and under your Mercury mount, one between the head and heart lines, indicates teaching skills and a calling to teach. Many small, parallel, vertical lines arising from horizontal relationship lines indicating children that are pupils may appear on the Mercury mount as well if your students are kids. *See also* teacher's square.

Medical stigmata: Five parallel lines on the mount of Mercury can indicate a healer.

Mercury finger: Your pinkie finger, having to do with communications, technology, and business deals.

Mercury mount: The fleshy lump just below your pinkie finger. *See also* Mercury finger.

Mercury rising line: A vertical line along the percussive edge of the hand pointing toward the pinkie finger, which has to do with communication.

Mixed: A hand shape that is a true mix of two or more hand shapes. A truly mixed hand will be very obvious, as if some fingers don't match others. In general, people with mixed hands are adaptable, and social, with many varied skills and hidden talents. Mixed hands are associated with the signs of Cancer, Aries, Gemini, and Pisces.

Mount: This word applies to the natural, fleshy lumps on the palms of the hands, including at the base of each finger and thumb and on the outer, percussive edge of the hand.

Mudra: A position in which the hands are held to have symbolic meaning, and to potentially encourage the flow of energy through meaningful spots on the hands.

Mystic cross: A cross under the middle finger, or below the junction between your middle finger and ring finger, shows intuition and a predisposition to study the occult.

Neptune mount: At the edge of the lunar mount at the bottom center of your palm, this area has to do with your dreams, both literal and figurative.

Nurse's lines: These vertical lines, found in groups above the heart line and below the fingers, are indications that the person has a healing touch. In addition to nursing, folks with nurse's lines would also make good massage therapists.

Omens: Signs seen in the world around you that indicate future events.

Overlay: Most often seen on the active hand, an overlay is the observation of rapidly changing hand features that seem to differ from the passive hand and from the usual way the active hand tends to look. An overlay also applies to features that don't fit with the rest of the hand pattern, such as small, delicate fingers on a beefy and rough hand.

Palmistry: Divination through the study of the hand's lines, shape, bone structure, flexibility, the fleshy parts of the palm and hand, skin, nails, and hair. Palmistry includes not only the palms of the hands, but also the backs of the hands and wrists.

Palm readers: People who have studied palmistry and can observe and interpret signs on the hand.

Passive Mars: Between the head and heart lines on the percussive edge of the hand, the passive Mars mount shows how you react to the world and people.

Percussive: The edge of your palm opposite your thumb, where you would strike if you were performing a karate chop.

Phalange: Any of the parts of the fingers or thumb in between the joints. Each finger naturally has three phalanges.

Philosophical: A hand shape typified by a long palm and long fingers that may be pointed and have pronounced joints and fleshy tips. Palms are oval shaped (broad in the center but narrowing at the top and bottom) and firm. Lines are numerous and deep. People with philosophical hands are often scholars, good at analysis, diplomatic, interested in culture and extravagance, and loners. Philosophical hands are associated with the signs of Aquarius and Capricorn.

Pinkie finger: *See* Mercury finger.

Pluto mount: A transient mount that may move around near where the middle of your palm meets your wrist. Your mount of Pluto has to do with karma and transformation in your life.

Poison line: Beginning on the percussive edge of the palm, very low on the lunar mount, a poison line is a horizontal line that juts across to the mount of Venus. This line can indicate a tendency toward allergies or addictions.

Practical: A hand shape that is generally square or a long rectangle with short and square fingers. Skin is often smooth and lines are deep. People with practical hands are consistent, earthy, patient, honest, detail-oriented, and decisive. Practical hands are associated with the signs of Capricorn and Virgo.

Protective square: A square found over a break in a line, especially the life line, that can indicate resources, strength, energy, and a period of isolation or confinement that helps a person get through a rough spot in life.

Psychic: A name given to the person or nature of fortune-telling using divination or simply the mind or spirit.

Psychic hand shape: A hand type that is long and slender with long fingers. Psychic palms are thin, smooth, and may be pale in color with many lines. People with psychic hands are generally idealists, intellectual, imaginative, and contemplative with a great deal of sensitivity and intuition. Psychic hands are associated with the signs of Aquarius and Pisces.

Psychic overlay: Features of a psychic hand type, like conic shape and long, thin fingers, mystic cross, thin skin, or branches on the head line that mark an otherwise ordinary hand as one of a psychic.

Psychometry: The practice of sensing energy from a hand or object by touch and feeling, rather than by looking at the features of the hand or object.

Quality: Line quality refers to the depth, length, and visibility of a line in the palm, including whether it looks like a shallow chain or a deep chasm.

Rajah loop: A loop starting at the junction between your pointer finger and middle finger, indicating royal ancestry and a charismatic person.

Rascettes: These bracelet lines on the wrist right below the palm are associated with several superstitions. The Romany believed that each line adds twenty-five years of longevity. The Greeks thought that when the top rascette arched up into the palm, it indicated difficulty in childbirth, and was the mark of one who was destined to be dedicated to the temple as a Vestal virgin.

Rhea: The tip phalange of the thumb, associated with will-power.

Ring of Saturn: A curved line cupping the mount of Saturn is an indication of a barrier to success.

Ring of Solomon: A curved line that cups the mount of Jupiter beneath the pointer finger. A ring of Solomon indicates an intuitive person drawn to psychic topics and psychology. A person with a ring of Solomon is also called to the service of humanity.

Rising line: A line that starts somewhere in the middle of your palm and goes straight up toward a finger. You can have a rising line for each finger, but some people have none, only one, or a few.

Saturn finger: Your middle finger, having to do with rules, authority figures, duties, career, and financial obligations.

Saturn mount: The fleshy lump below your middle finger. *See also* Saturn finger.

Saturn rising line: *See* destiny line.

Set: The set of a finger is how high it sits relative to other fingers as attached to the palm when your hand is held vertically upright in front of your face.

Simian crease: A fused heart and head line, indicating a stubborn person who is of one mind and purpose.

Sister line: A parallel line, usually referring to one shadowing the life line, shows strength. It can sometimes indicate leading a double life, especially if another sister line shadows the heart line.

Spatulate: A hand shape characterized by a generally square or wide rectangular palm that may be broader at the fingers. Fingers are long with flattened tips and sometimes wide joints. Palms of spatulate hands are thick and substantial, and lines are deep and well-defined. People with spatulate palms are likable, social, competent, and confident and may be mechanically and spatially inclined. Spatulate hands are associated with the signs of Sagittarius, Capricorn, and Gemini.

Square: A source of stability and strength, squares can be viewed as positive, but they also represent a period of necessary sequestering away from the world, which can be anything from a happy spiritual retreat to jail time.

Star: An asterisk, pentagram, or Star of David in the palm indicates a focus point for conflict.

Sun line: Also known as a rising line to Apollo or a sister line to the destiny line. This line is a positive sign, indicating confidence and success.

Sympathy line: A horizontal straight line found on the mount of Jupiter directly below the pointer finger. People with a sympathy line are very understanding and tolerant.

Tassel: Multiple fraying forks found at the end of the hepatica or life line, associated with the decay of health found during old age.

Teacher's square: A square found on or just below the mount of Jupiter is a sign of a good teacher. *See also* mark of the teacher.

Thumb: Your thumb has to do with your flexibility and your willpower.

Triangle: In general, a source of strength, energy, and "good" karma.

Triangle of earnings: Formed from the head line, the destiny line, and a Mercury line, a sign of money coming, depending upon the size of the triangle. Bigger is better.

Trident: Three lines diverging from one another, indicating a decision point that may be tricky, but can lead to better things.

Ulnar loop: A loop starting on the percussive edge of the hand and jutting onto the lunar mount, indicating a person in touch with their subconscious and with nature.

Uranus mount: At the edge of your lunar mount, the plain of Mars, and passive Mars, your mount of Uranus has to do with inventiveness and how you build upon your ideals.

Venusian line: *See* life line.

Venus mount: At the base of the thumb, your mount of Venus shows your love energy in life. The mount of Venus is also the third or base phalange of the thumb.

Via lascivia: A horizontal curving line from the junction of your pointer and middle fingers up to the ring finger or the junction between it and your pinkie finger, having to do with passion and sensuality.

Vulcan: *See* active Mars.

Water: A hand shape with a long rectangular or oval palm and long fingers. People with water hands are artistic, imaginative, emotional, and sensitive.

Whorl: Fingerprints are great examples of whorls, but they can be found anywhere on the skin of the palm (and feet). They consist of small, swirling lines best seen in an ink print or with a magnifying glass.

Worry lines: Small lines, often numerous, radiating out from the base of the thumb on the mount of Venus. Worry lines can affect health in the future when they cross the life line on the active hand.

Writer's fork: A fork at the end of the head line that is conducive to coming up with good ideas for writing or creating in words.

BIBLIOGRAPHY

Bulfinch, Thomas. *Bulfinch's Greek and Roman Mythology: The Age of Fable.* Mineola, NY: 1859.

Cheiro. *Cheiro's Palmistry for All: A Practical Work on the Study of the Lines of the Hand.* New York: Arco Pub., 1982.

Cunningham, Scott. *Divination for Beginners.* St. Paul, MN: Llewellyn Publications, 2003.

Gile, Robin, and Lisa Lenard. *The Complete Idiot's Guide to Palmistry.* Indianapolis, IN: Alpha Books, 1999.

Graves, Robert. *The White Goddess: A Historical Grammar of Poetic Myth, Amended and Enlarged Edition.* New York: Farrar, Straus, and Giroux, 1948.

Hazel, Peter. *Palmistry Quick & Easy*. Woodbury, MN: Llewellyn Publications, 2009.

Kynes, Sandra. *Change at Hand: Balancing Your Energy Through Palmistry, Chakras, and Mudras*. Woodbury, MN: Llewellyn Publications, 2009.

Saint-Germain, Jon. *Lover's Guide to Palmistry: Finding Love in the Palm of Your Hand*. Woodbury, MN: Llewellyn Publications, 2008.

Webster, Richard. *Palm Reading for Beginners: Find Your Future in the Palm of Your Hand*. Woodbury, MN: Llewellyn Publications, 2008.

West, Peter. *The Complete Illustrated Guide to Palmistry: The Principles and Practice of Hand Reading Revealed*. Shaftesbury, Dorset, UK: Element Books Limited, 1998.

APPENDIX:
HAND STUDIES

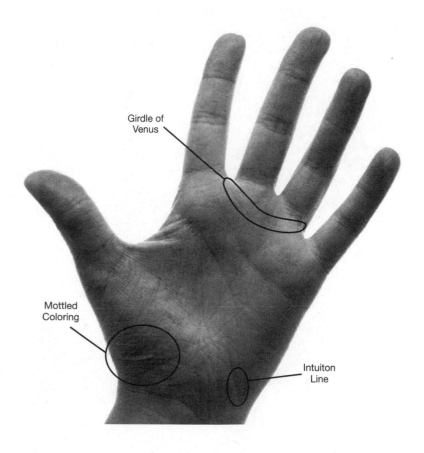

Girdle of
Venus

Mottled
Coloring

Intuiton
Line

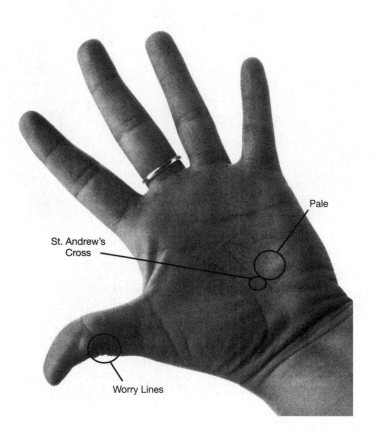

Pale

St. Andrew's
Cross

Worry Lines

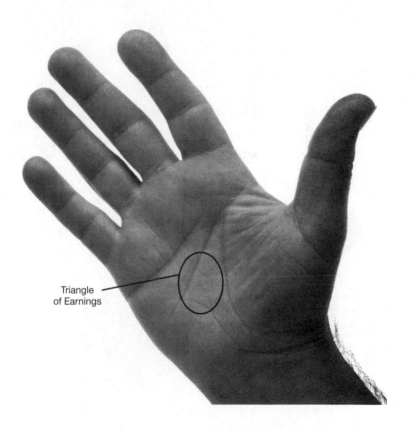

Triangle
of Earnings

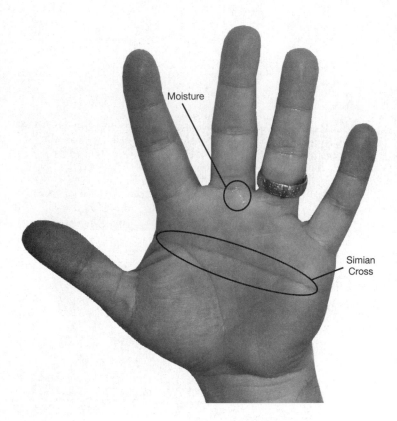

Moisture

Simian
Cross

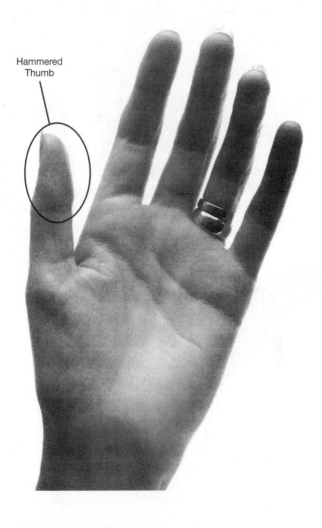

Hammered
Thumb

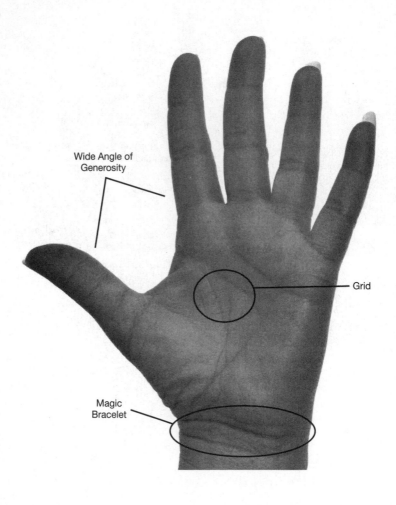

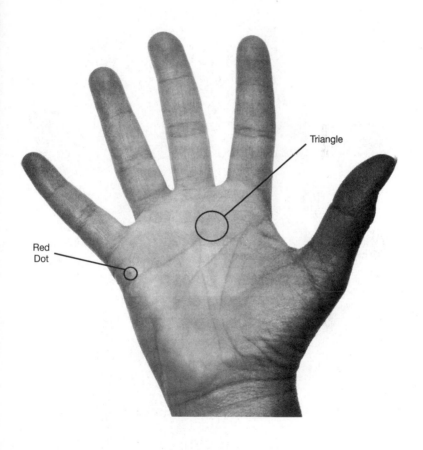

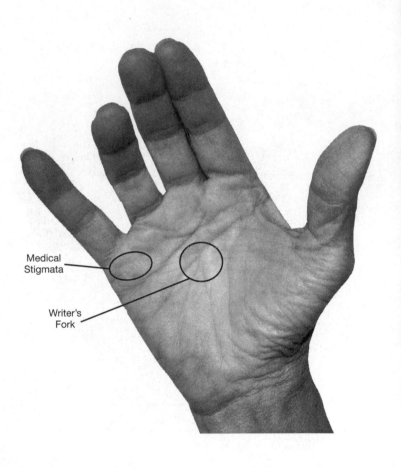

Medical
Stigmata

Writer's
Fork

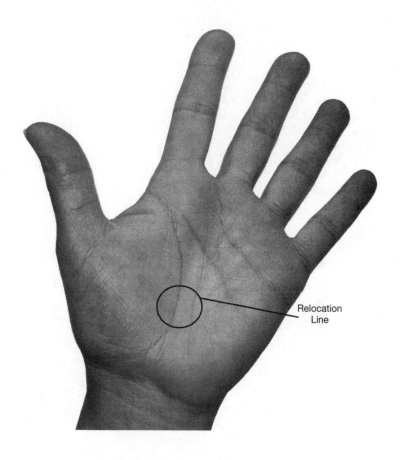

Relocation
Line

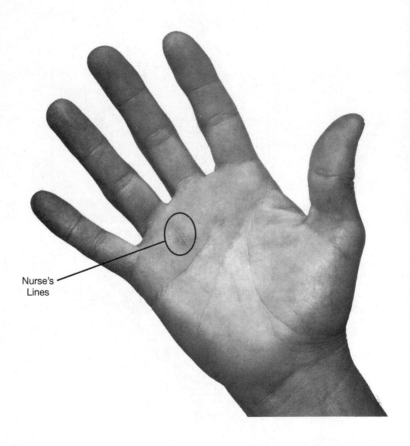

Nurse's
Lines

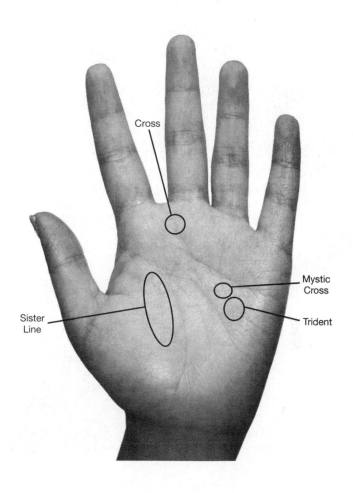

Cross

Mystic
Cross

Sister
Line

Trident

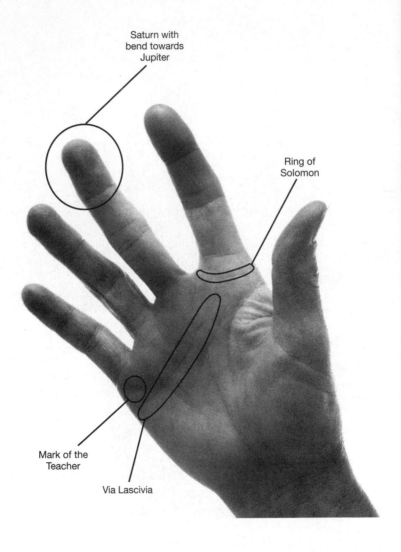

Saturn with
bend towards
Jupiter

Ring of
Solomon

Mark of the
Teacher

Via Lascivia

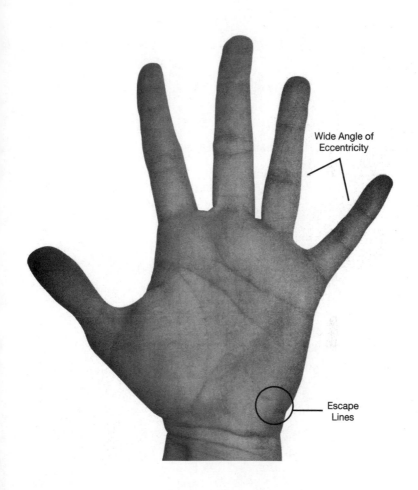

Wide Angle of
Eccentricity

Escape
Lines

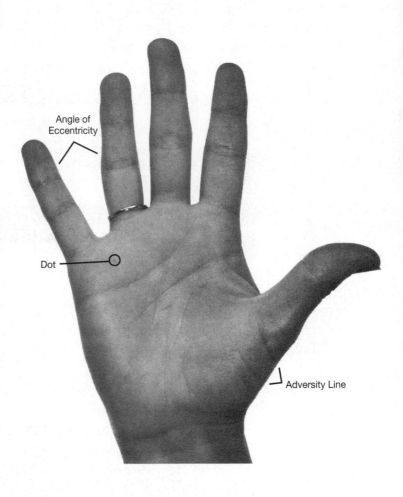

Angle of
Eccentricity

Dot

Adversity Line

Crystal Ball Reading
Reading

For Beginners

Easy Divination & Interpretation

ALEXANDRA CHAURAN

Crystal Ball Reading for Beginners
Easy Divination & Interpretation
ALEXANDRA CHAURAN

Anyone can learn to use a crystal ball for divination, guidance, and meditation. This friendly introductory guide, written by a second-generation fortune-teller, is the only book available that focuses solely on the benefits of crystal ball reading. The author, a professional reader, presents everything you need to know to begin doing crystal ball readings immediately. You'll learn what a crystal ball is, how it works, and how to choose your first one. Step-by-step instructions describe what to look for when doing a reading and how to interpret the symbols found within the crystal ball. You can gain heightened intuitive abilities, greater self-knowledge, and a deeper understanding of the universe when you practice the ancient art of crystal ball reading.

978-0-7387-2626-7, 216 pp., 5³⁄₁₆ x 8   **$14.95**

So
You
Want
to Be
a
PSYCHIC
INTUITIVE?

A Down-to-Earth Guide

Alexandra Chauran

So You Want to Be a Psychic Intuitive?
A Down-to-Earth Guide
Alexandra Chauran

Dependable guidance, communication with departed loved ones, helping friends and family—the lifelong rewards of a strong psychic connection are countless. Whether you're a beginner or already in touch with your intuition, this encouraging, conversational, and hands-on guide can help you strengthen your psychic skills. Featuring illustrative anecdotes and easy exercises, you'll learn how to achieve a receptive state, identify your source of information, receive messages, and interpret coincidences, dreams, and symbols. Step-by-step instructions make it easy to try a variety of psychic techniques and divination, such as telepathy, channeling, spirit communication, automatic writing, and scrying. There's also practical advice for wisely applying your enhanced psychic skills personally and professionally.

978-0-7387-3065-3, 264 pp., 5³⁄₁₆ x 8 **$14.95**

High Forehead
Shows he's intelligent and has an active mind

Dilated Pupils
Eyes express interest in each other

Small Nostrils
Shows she's cautious

Sensual Lips
Mutual interest in each other

Face Reading
QUICK & EASY

Richard Webster

Face Reading Quick & Easy
Richard Webster

Based on ancient Chinese wisdom similar to palmistry and acupuncture, face reading teaches us to really see the faces we look at every day. Learn how the zones of the face reveal personality characteristics, and how meaning is hidden in our features. Includes exercises designed to help you read the fortunes, struggles, and triumphs written on your own face and those of friends, family, colleagues, and business contacts. Also included are helpful tips for reading emotional cues during important meetings, like job interviews, and tips for recognizing when a person is lying, as popularized on television with the "human lie detector" phenomenon.

978-0-7387-3296-1, 264 pp., 6 x 9   **$16.99**

Divination

For Beginners

Reading the Past, Present & Future

SCOTT CUNNINGHAM

Divination for Beginners
Reading the Past, Present & Future
SCOTT CUNNINGHAM

There's no need to visit a soothsayer or call a psychic hotline to glimpse into your future or to uncover your past. You can become your own diviner of things unseen with the many methods outlined in this book, written by popular author Scott Cunningham.

Here you will find detailed descriptions of both common and unusual divinatory techniques, each grouped by the tools or techniques used to perform them. Many utilize natural forces such as water, clouds, smoke, and the movement of birds. Also discussed are the more advanced techniques of Tarot, Palmistry, and the I Ching.

978-0-7387-0384-8, 264 pp., 5³⁄₁₆ x 8   **$13.95**

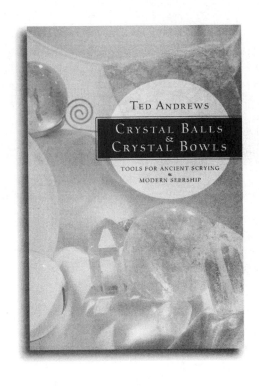

TED ANDREWS

CRYSTAL BALLS
&
CRYSTAL BOWLS

TOOLS FOR ANCIENT SCRYING
&
MODERN SEERSHIP

Crystal Balls & Crystal Bowls
Tools for Ancient Scrying & Modern Seership
TED ANDREWS

Quartz crystal balls and crystal bowls are popular magical tools. Yet, not everyone understands the extent of their power and multipurpose potential. Ted Andrews reveals how these dynamic instruments can be used for divination, astral projection, spirit communication, healing, and reaching higher states of consciousness.

Readers will learn many methods of crystal gazing, along with ways to enhance this practice with candles, fragrances, and elixirs. Also included are techniques for divining with water, communicating with angels and spirit guides, developing clairvoyance, and activating creativity. This updated edition also contains new illustrations.

978-1-5671-8026-8, 256 pp., 6 x 9   **$16.99**

To order, call 1-877-NEW-WRLD
Prices subject to change without notice
Order at Llewellyn.com 24 hours a day, 7 days a week!